Lecture Notes in Computer Science   11609

More information about this series at http://www.springer.com/series/7409

Marco Brambilla · Cinzia Cappiello ·
Siew Hock Ow (Eds.)

Current Trends in Web Engineering

ICWE 2019 International Workshops
DSKG, KDWEB, MATWEP
Daejeon, South Korea, June 11, 2019
Proceedings

 Springer

Editors
Marco Brambilla ⓘ
Dipartimento di Elettronica,
Informazione e Bioingegneria
Politecnico di Milano
Milan, Italy

Cinzia Cappiello ⓘ
Dipartimento di Elettronica,
Informazione e Bioingegneria
Politecnico di Milano
Milan, Italy

Siew Hock Ow ⓘ
Department of Software Engineering
University of Malaya
Kuala Lumpur, Malaysia

ISSN 0302-9743   ISSN 1611-3349   (electronic)
Lecture Notes in Computer Science
ISBN 978-3-030-51252-1   ISBN 978-3-030-51253-8   (eBook)
https://doi.org/10.1007/978-3-030-51253-8

LNCS Sublibrary: SL3 – Information Systems and Applications, incl. Internet/Web, and HCI

This Springer imprint is published by the registered company Springer Nature Switzerland AG
The registered company address is: Gewerbestrasse 11, 6330 Cham, Switzerland

Preface

This volume collects the papers presented at the workshops co-located with the 19th International Conference on Web Engineering (ICWE 2019), held on June 11, in Daejeon, South Korea. The objective of the conference is to bring together researchers and practitioners from various disciplines in academia and industry to address and discuss the emerging challenges in the engineering of Web applications and associated technologies, as well as to assess the impact of these technologies on society, media, and culture.

As in previous years, the conference main program was complemented by a number of co-located workshops that provided a forum for participants to discuss novel and cutting-edge topics, both within the Web Engineering community and at the crossroads with other communities. We accepted the following three workshops, whose papers are included in this volume after they underwent a rigorous peer-review process and were presented during the workshops on June 11, 2019.

- International Workshop on Data Science and Knowledge Graph (DSKG 2019)
- 5th International Workshop on Knowledge Discovery on the Web (KDWEB 2019)
- Second International Workshop on Maturity of Web Engineering Practices (MATWEP 2019)

The DSKG workshop aims to share and discuss knowledge graph techniques based on open data, with methods coming both from academia and industry. The workshop includes five papers.

The KDWEB workshop, featuring four papers, focuses on the field of knowledge discovery from digital data, with particular attention for advanced data mining, machine learning, and information retrieval methods, systems, and applications.

The MATWEP workshop provides an open discussion space, starting from the two accepted papers and combining solid theory work with practical on-the-field experience in the Web Engineering area, with the general aim of assessing the maturity of the field.

We would like to thank everyone who contributed to the ICWE 2019 workshops. First, we thank the workshop organizers for their excellent work in identifying cutting-edge and cross-disciplinary topics in the rapidly moving field of Web Engineering, and organizing inspiring workshops around them. Secondly, we thank the conference organizers and hosts.

A word of thanks goes also to the reviewers who provided thorough evaluations of the papers and contributed to the promotion of the workshops. Last, but not least, we thank all the authors who submitted to and presented papers at the workshops for having shared their work with the community and contributing to the success of these events.

June 2019

Marco Brambilla
Cinzia Cappiello
Siew Hock Ow

Contents

**Second International Workshop on Maturity
of Web Engineering Practices (MATWEP 2019)**

International Workshop on Data Science and Knowledge Graph (DSKG)

International Workshop on Data Science and Knowledge Graph

This volume contains the proceedings of the **International Workshop on Data Science and Knowledge Graph**, co-located with the 19th International Conference on Web Engineering (ICWE 2019) and held on June 11, 2019, in Daejeon, South Korea.

Obtaining a primary data source is critical to construct a knowledge graph, since building a new knowledge from scratch is not trivial. Recently, significant amounts of data are published as open data in research, commercial and governments. This workshop shares broad topics including knowledge population using open data. In particular, the participants discuss knowledge graph techniques based on open data such as data wrangling, big data analysis, data visualization, and knowledge transformation both academia and industries.

Following the call for papers, 11 authors submitted their papers for presentation at the workshop. Of these, the program committee carefully selected a total of 5 papers which you will find bundled in this volume:

- Su-Seong Chai and Dongjun Suh
  A Design of Building Inventory for Risk Analysis using Open Data
- Jangwon Gim
  Technical invention trend analysis of applicants based on CPC classification
- Yuchul Jung
  A Study on Automatic Keyphrase Extraction and its Refinement for Scientific Articles
- Min Jung Lee, Jiyoung Woo
  A Study on the Characteristics of the Long-term Web Forum Users using Social Network Analysis
- Haklae Kim
  Knowledge Exploration from Tables on the Web

The workshop program also featured a panel discussion about creating a national data map of the Government. The Korean government has released various datasets with their metadata, and plans to construct a knowledge graph for interlinking the released datasets. In our discussion, the participants provide various opinions for achieving these objectives.

Our sincere thanks go to all authors for their interest in the workshop and to the members of the program committee for their insightful and careful reviews, all of which were prepared on a tight schedule but still received in time. All of you have helped to make the International Workshop on Data Science and Knowledge Graph a successful event.

June 2019

Haklae Kim
Jangwon Gim
Yuchul Jung

DSKG 2019 Organization

Workshop Chairs

Haklae Kim   Chung-Ang University, Seoul, South Korea
Jangwon Gim   Kunsan National University, Jeollabuk-do, South Korea
Yuchul Jung   Kumoh National Institute of Technology, Gyeongsangbuk-do,
                  South Korea

A Design of Building Inventory for Risk Analysis Using Open Data

Su-Seong Chai[1] and Dongjun Suh[2(✉)]

[1] Korea Institute of Science and Technology Information,
245 Daehak-ro, Yuseong-gu, Daejeon 34141, South Korea
sschai@kisti.re.kr
[2] School of Convergence and Fusion System Engineering,
Kyungpook National University (KNU), 2559, Gyeongsang-daero,
Sangju-si, Gyeongsangbuk-do 37224, South Korea
dongjunsuh@knu.ac.kr

Abstract. This study introduces a design of building inventory for risk analysis using open data in Korea. Recently, disasters of various sizes and types are occurring globally. Risk analysis tools are used to estimate the losses due to disasters. However, there is a limitation in the application of disaster statistical data in Korea because these data are based on the country where the tool is produced. To improve the accuracy of loss assessment, it is necessary to utilize data in consideration of each country's environment. However, the data opened at the national level are distributed among various organizations. Thus, considerable time is required to build infrastructure. Therefore, we collect the open data distributed among various institutions and ensure data compatibility and interoperability through the standardization of the data in various formats. In addition to a disaster analysis system, a design method for a database system that can support various analysis systems through the data is proposed considering scalability.

Keywords: Open data · Risk analysis · Building inventory · Disaster · Database system

1 Introduction

Various types of large-scale disasters have been occurring continuously, and flood damage and fire-related earthquake damage have increased. In Korea, which is regarded as a safe earthquake, there were earthquakes in Gyeongju (magnitude of 5.8) and Pohang (magnitude of 5.4) in 2016 and 2017, respectively. Therefore, it is necessary to develop technologies that can comprehensively predict and deal with various disasters that occur at multiple levels at the national level and to increase resilience against disasters [1].

HAZUS-MH, ERGO, SYNER-G [2–4] are representative tools used for earthquake analysis. Most of such tools calculate building damage from earthquakes, assess damage and losses, and calculate the number of refugees and shelters required based on

M. Brambilla et al. (Eds.): ICWE 2019 Workshops, LNCS 11609, pp. 5–9, 2020.
https://doi.org/10.1007/978-3-030-51253-8_1

the degree of damage. Data that provide information about damaged areas are required to perform loss assessment.

In South Korea, disaster damage statistics, relevant research data, and actual measurement data are being studied. However, in the case of earthquakes, there is lack of data to estimate loss assessment. Therefore, the analysis is based on the actual earthquake-related data provided by HAZUS-MH, which is a loss assessment tool of the Federal Emergency Management Agency (FEMA), and research from abroad.

The earthquake-related data provided by HAZUS-MH and the weight data used in loss assessment reflect the environment and conditions of the country concerned. Therefore, to carry out the loss assessment for the Korean environment, data appropriate to this environment are required. Loss assessment uses a variety of data such as demographic figures and building integration information. The data surveyed at the national level (open data) are managed by public authorities and public data portals [5]. However, these data are distributed among institutions, and considerable time is required to build research infrastructure. In addition, the data are composed of various formats such as structured and unstructured data. Thus, it is necessary to ensure data compatibility and interoperability through data standardization.

In this study, we construct a database system by collecting distributed open data, standardizing the data by considering characteristics, and refining the data in a structured and compatible format. The constructed database system serves as a data platform, and it can provide data suitable for the Korean environment. Researchers and decision makers can assist in the disaster risk analysis process including loss assessment. We propose a database system construction method that integrates the data used in various types of loss assessment such as population and economic losses. The rest of this paper is organized as follows: Sect. 2 describes the overseas technologies used for estimating disaster losses. Section 3 explains the method of constructing the database system. Finally, Sect. 4 provides the conclusions and the direction of future research.

2 Related Works

HAZUS-MH is a software platform developed by the FEMA to assess natural disaster risk. Assuming the occurrence of a disaster, it predicts the extent of damage and helps in planning and strategizing to reduce risk. When an earthquake occurs, direct or indirect damage is caused by the loss of infrastructure, such as residential and commercial buildings, the loss of production facilities owing to physical losses, the resulting economic losses including the cost of discontinuing production and restoration costs, social losses from casualties and shelter supply, and indirect economic losses such as the input of national budget.

The National Center for Supercomputing Applications in Illinois is responsible for the research and development of ERGO. ERGO is an open-source-based complex disaster risk assessment tool that is open to all users and therefore easy to access and scalable. If a data inventory is built for each country's environment, such as buildings, housing, transportation, and lifeline data, the inventory can be used to assess loss and to estimate damage considering the state of the country.

3 Complex Disaster Loss Assessment Analysis Database System

Data suitable for the Korean environment were collected to construct a complex disaster loss assessment analysis system for South Korea. A standardized database was designed by collecting and refining the data distributed in public institutions. The design of the database considers extensibility, and loaded data can be utilized as open data in various analysis systems including disaster analysis systems. Figure 1 shows the ER diagram of the complex disaster loss assessment and damage analysis database system designed in this study.

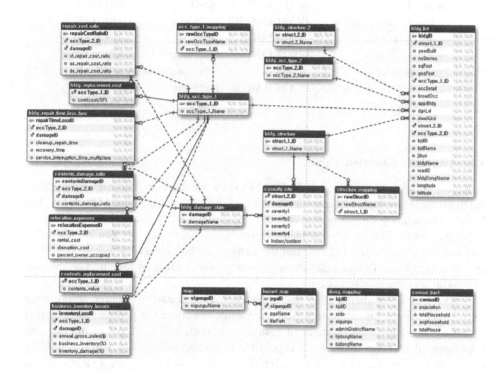

Fig. 1. ER diagram of loss estimation database system

3.1 Building-Related Table

The related data to be loaded on building tables are provided as open data in the national spatial information portal of the Ministry of Land, Transport and Maritime Affairs [6]. One building contains various types of attribute information, as shown in Table 1. Building information data are the basis for estimating risk and loss in complex disasters that occur in a series of earthquake events. The damage caused by disasters includes economic and human losses, and it mostly occurs in buildings. The magnitude of an earthquake has the largest impact on the physical damage to buildings. Attribute information, such as the structure and uses of a building, can be used primarily to estimate the degree of damage to the building and to predict and estimate the damage resulting from population and economic losses. A building's appraisal value and the value of contents can be used to estimate economic loss, and population loss can be estimated based on the occupants of the building. As the attribute information of a building is fixed, it is possible to construct a table. In addition, the use of the latest data increases the accuracy of damage loss assessment and prediction results.

Table 1. Main columns of building table

Table	Column	Type	Column	Type
Bldg_list	bldgID(P.K)	VARCHAR(30)	bjdID	VARCHAR(30)
	Struct_1_ID(F.K)	VARCHAR(30)	bjdNAme	VARCHAR(30)
	yearBuilt	SMALLINT	Jibun	VARCHAR(30)
	noStories	SMALLINT	bldgName	VARCHAR(30)
	sqFoot	FLOAT	bldgDongName	VARCHAR(30)
	occType_1_ID(F.K)	VARCHAR(30)	longitude	FLOAT
	apprBldg	INT	latitude	FLOAT

3.2 Population-Related Table

In Korea, population data can be obtained based on the demographic data provided by the Statistical Geographic Information Service of the National Statistical Office [7]. The National Population Census is a survey of the National Statistical Office; it is conducted every five years. The survey can identify population trends such as gender, age, educational level, sex, marital status, and the number of households. The census is conducted using census output area, which is the minimum statistical zone unit established to provide statistical information.

Table 2 is a population table that shows output area and population information data, which are the minimum statistical zone units. Based on the population table, it is necessary to identify the number of residents in each building. By identifying the population of each building unit, it is possible to predict the casualties in the building and predict and evaluate the loss of the building when a disaster occurs. In addition, the number of victims seeking shelter can be estimated by identifying casualties to control the accommodation of shelters and to establish additional shelters. However, as the minimum unit of population information is output area, it is necessary to study the population information of buildings. Considering that the proportion of high-rise buildings is large in South Korea and the number of apartments is larger than that of single-family houses, the accuracy of estimating the population of buildings is a considerably important factor in estimating population loss.

The population table is composed of county ID, population, total households, average households, and the total number of houses. However, it does not include attribute information such as gender, age, population, single-person households, and two-person households. When the data of output area are missing from the various types of attribute information, a process of refining the attribute information of missing parts is additionally required.

Table 2. Main columns of population table

Table	Column	Type
Census_Tract	censusID(P.K)	VARCHAR(20)
	Population	INT
	totalHousehold	INT
	avgHousehold	INT
	totalHouse	INT

4   Conclusion

The building inventory database system proposed in this study will be provided to the researchers of disaster response prediction and analysis systems for investigating future complex disaster response in Korea. This can support decision making to predict the scale and extent of damage and to minimize damage. In future, we will collect the geological and weight data of Korea and expand the functions of ERGO to construct and analyze a complex disaster loss assessment database suitable for the South Korean environment.

Acknowledgement. This work was supported by the National Research Foundation of Korea (NRF) grant funded by the Korea government (MSIT) (No. 2018R1C1B5084507).

References

1. Chai, S.-S., Shin, S., Suh, D.: A study on the development of korean inventory for the multi-hazard risk assessment. J. Dig. Contents Soc. **18**(6), 1127–1134 (2017)
2. HAZUS-MH 2.1 Technical Manual, Department of Homeland Security Federal Emergency Management Agency, Washington, D.C., Technical Manual 2.1
3. ERGO, http://ergo.ncsa.illinois.edu/?page_id=44. Accessed 29 Apr 2019
4. SYNER-G, http://www.vce.at/SYNER-G/. Accessed 29 Apr 2019
5. Open Data Portal. https://www.data.go.kr. Accessed 29 Apr 2019
6. National Special Data Infrastructure Portal. http://www.nsdi.go.kr/. Accessed 29 Apr 2019
7. Korean Statistical Information Service. http://kosis.kr/. Accessed 29 Apr 2019

Technical Invention Trend Analysis of Applicants Based on CPC Classification

Jiyee Jeon, Soohyeon Chae, and Jangwon Gim$^{(\boxtimes)}$

Kunsan National University, Gunsan-si, Jeollabuk-do 54150, South Korea
{nayajiyee,soohyeon,jwgim}@kunsan.ac.kr

Abstract. Recently, with the rapid development of science and technology, new technologies are rapidly emerging, and applicants are making efforts to acquire intellectual property rights to prevail the competitive advantage of technology and enhance technological competitiveness. As a result, the number of patents invented increases rapidly every year, and the ripple effects of the developed technologies are also increasing in terms of social and economic aspects. Therefore, applicants are focusing on evaluating the value of existing invented technologies to invent more valuable technologies. Although existing patent analysis studies mainly focus on discovering core technologies among the technologies derived from patents or analyzing trend changes for specific techniques. Therefore, the analysis of applicants who develop such core technologies is insufficient. In this paper, we propose a model for analyzing the technical inventions of applicants based on CPC classification codes. Through the proposed model, the common invention patterns of applicants are extracted, and the technical inventions of applicants are analyzed using the patterns. We prove that applicants have different invention patterns and trends in inventing technologies.

Keywords: Applicant analysis · Technical invention pattern · CPC Classification

1 Introduction

In the era of the Fourth Industrial Revolution, new technologies are rapidly being invented, and inventors are making great efforts to claim rights to sources and core technologies [1,2]. Among the various forms of intellectual property rights, the patent literature typically includes the rights of the applicant's core or base techniques, so that a company or inventor can claim rights to the technologies based on the patent literature. Therefore, studies are being conducted to extract key technologies through mining and analysis of the terms specified in

J. Gim—This work was supported by the National Research Foundation of Korea (NRF) grant funded by the Korea government (MSIT) (No. NRF-2018R1C1B6008624).

© Springer Nature Switzerland AG 2020
M. Brambilla et al. (Eds.): ICWE 2019 Workshops, LNCS 11609, pp. 10–17, 2020.
https://doi.org/10.1007/978-3-030-51253-8_2

the patent documents, and to analyze the life cycle of the extracted technology values and technologies [3–9]. For this purpose, existing patent analysis methods focus on the patent technical terms expressed in the patent literature. Therefore, researches were conducted to extract the core technologies of the inventor and analyze the value of the derived technologies by mining the terms specified in the patent literature. These studies focused on the extraction of patented technical terms using natural language processing and text mining techniques, but patents guarantee novelty and inventiveness to the rights of the technology. Thus, the vocabularies specified in the new patent document contains in newly defined terms or similar alternative terms. For this reason, the recall rate is low when searching for core technologies from patents. Therefore, the EU and the US Patent Office have proposed a new classification system, CPC, to improve the retrieval performance and classification accuracy of patent documents. Although the IPC classification system has already been defined for the patent classification, the IPC classification system has limitations in classifying new technologies or classifying the technologies at a detailed level. CPC, on the other hand, is adding a new domain (Y-section) and can be categorized into a more detailed and broader range of technologies than the IPC, including more than 260,000 detailed taxonomies. Besides, since 2013, CPC codes have been granted to patents invented in the European Union, the United States, and the Republic of Korea, and the CPC classification system plays a vital role in global patent analysis. However, since most of the related researches focus on the analysis of technology and the trend of the invention, analysis of the technical value of the inventor or the institution that invented the technology is insufficient. Therefore, in this paper, we propose an analytic method that can help to establish a patent strategy by deriving the core technology possessed by the applicant based on the advanced patent classification system and conducting a case study on the applicant's change in invention trend. The composition of this paper is as follows. Section 2 discusses the limitations of previous studies and the necessity of this study. In Sect. 3, we describe a method for extracting patented invention pattern based on the proposed model. The results of case analysis by the applicant based on the proposed model are described in Sect. 4, and conclusions and future studies are described in Sect. 5.

2   Related Work

The existing related studies for patent analysis can be roughly classified into analysis methods considering the structural characteristics of patent documents and methods of analyzing technical terms specified in patent documents. By analyzing the technology trends of the technology, it is possible to identify the technology of the competitors by extracting the patent technical terms and establish the technology development strategy. Research has been conducted to predict trends [4–6]. These studies use patent text mining and natural language processing techniques to analyze patents on technical terms included in patents. However, since a patented invention must have novelty and inventive step, terms expressed in the patent literature can be derived in a similar form. Therefore, the recall rate of patent searches using technical terms is low. A patent analysis method based on a patent classification system was studied to systematically carry out the technical classification considering the features of these patents. [7] proposes a social network analysis (SNA) method based on IPC classification system to extract core technology. [8] uses IPC to analyze associative analysis and social network analysis methods to analyze the technology trends of related technologies and related technologies, extract the relationship. [9] proposed technology convergence analysis technique by deriving the convergence technology domain by applying an association rule mining technique based on CPC classification scheme. However, existing studies do not consider the technical classification at a detailed level, and concentrate on core technology extraction and analysis. In this paper, we propose a method of extracting the applicant's invention pattern based on the CPC classification system and analyzing the invention's trend by an applicant.

3   Proposed Model

The proposed model consists of four steps as the Fig. 1. To analyze invention trends of applicants', the first step is to collect patent data and extract the desired information from the collected data. We acquire raw data using OpenAPI from Korea Intellectual Property Rights Information Service (KIPRIS) which provides information service on patent data invented in Korea. Patent metadata and specific information such as title, claim, abstract, invention date, publication date, etc. are extracted from original patent documents. In the second preprocessing process, patent data are clustered based on time series information (date of invention, year of publication) for the applicant's invention transition analysis. In the third step, common patterns are extracted from the experimental data using the patent classification system CPC. Based on the common pattern extracted at the final step, the applicant's invention trend is analyzed. Through the above four steps, we will compare and analyze the trends of patent inventions for various applicants such as University, Company, and Institute. To analyze applicant invention trends, a common pattern based on the CPC classification system is defined as shown in Table 1.

Table 1. Pattern of invention (S), (T), (E), (I) definition

Pattern of invention	Equation	Definition
Same (S)	$Code_1 = Code_2$	The same CPC codes on the sub-group level
Transition (T)	$Code_1 = Code_2$	Change the CPC codes on the sub-group level
Expansion (E)	$Code_1 \rightarrow Code_2$	Change the CPC codes on the main-group level
Independent (I)	$Code_1 \rightarrow Code_2$	Change the CPC codes on the sub-class level

Figure 2 shows an example of analyzing the applicant's invention pattern based on the common pattern defined in Table 1. To analyze the applicant's

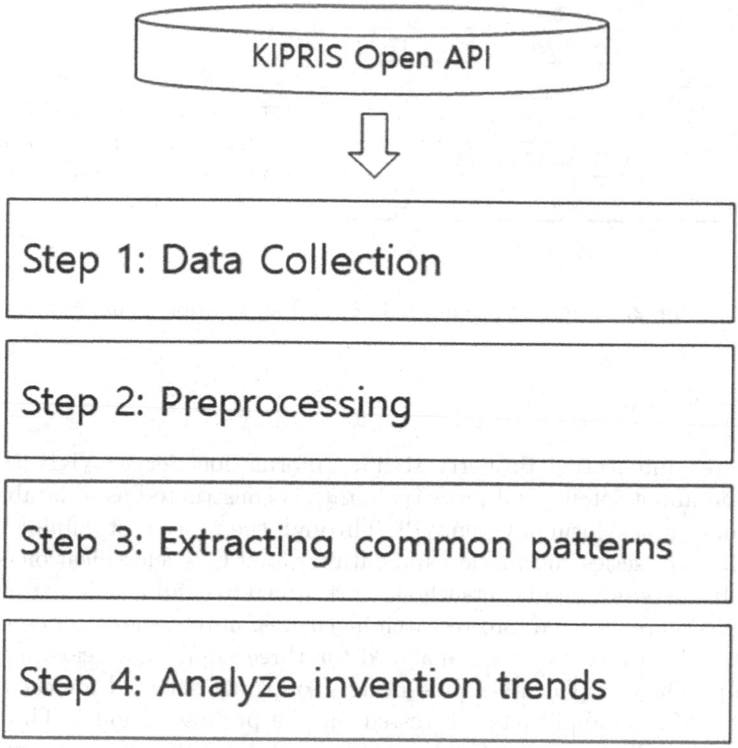

Step 1: Data Collection

Step 2: Preprocessing

Step 3: Extracting common patterns

Step 4: Analyze invention trends

Fig. 1. Overall process for analyzing patterns of inventors

invention trend, patent information invented by year is grouped, and the CPC codes among the patents are compared. One patent includes at least one CPC classification code and extracts a common pattern from the CPC classification codes included in the comparative patents. For example, in the comparison patent PT_1, PT_2 comparison pair, PT_1 is defined as a prior patent and PT_2 as a follow patent. At this time, the same (S) pattern is defined when the CPC classification codes of PT_1 and PT_2 are the same up to the subgroup level. Therefore, 'G06F 17/30' and 'G06F 17/30', which appeared in patents invented in 2007, are defined to be the same (S) relation because the subgroups are the same. Also, since the 'G06F 17/30' in 2007 and 'G06F 17/18' in 2009 are related to the subgroups of the CPC classification code, the following patent is regarded as a transition of some of the prior patent. Expansion (E) means that the classification code of the subsequent patents is different from that of the prior patent and the main group. It is an extension relationship between 'G06F 17/30' in 2007 and 'G06F 50/18' in 2008. Also, 'G06F 17/30' in 2007 and 'H04L 63/30' in 2008 are defined as a mutually independent (I) relationship, considering that there is no mutual intersection in terms of technology classification.

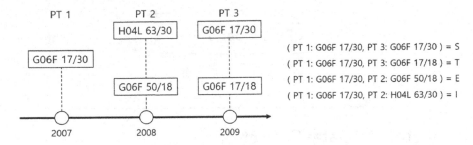

Fig. 2. Pattern of invention S, T, E, I application example

4   Experiment

In the Korea Intellectual Property Rights Information Service (KIPRIS), the information about intellectual property rights is constructed as a database and provides data in the form of Open API. Through the process of refining the collected data, time series information and data without CPC classification code are removed. In this study, applicants who are presumed to exhibit different inventive characteristics are grouped into research institutes, universities, and companies, and the trends of inventions are analyzed for three applicants belonging to the each group. Three applicants representing groups are selected for each group, and a total of nine applicants are tested on the proposed model. The Table 2 represents the collected and refined experimental data statistical information.

Table 2. Experimental data set for each applicant group containing CPC code

Group	Organization	Total patents	Number of refined CPC
Institute	I_1	293	252
	I_2	628	1,142
	I_3	1,048	1,213
Company	C_1	269	165
	C_2	366	436
	C_3	655	331
University	U_1	3,672	4,908
	U_2	3,603	4,841
	U_3	4,908	4,423

Tables 3, 4 and 5 show the experiment results that contain common pattern ratios extracted from each group. Table 3 shows the S, T, E, and I patterns derived from the three applicants belonging to the institute.

Table 4 shows the results of the three applicants representing the company. The three applicants have significantly higher Expansion (E) patterns than the

Table 3. Experiment result of Institutes based on common patterns

Institute						
Pattern of invention	I_1		I_2		I_3	
	Frequency	Rate	Frequency	Rate	Frequency	Rate
Same	20,422	5.31	11,949	0.28	73,619	0.66
Transition	28,278	7.35	59,916	1.42	186,095	1.68
Expansion	84,235	21.91	165,533	3.91	981,317	8.85
Independent	251,559	65.43	3,974,732	94.36	9,847,974	88.81

Table 4. Experiment result of Companies based on common patterns

Company						
Pattern of invention	C_1		C_2		C_3	
	Frequency	Rate	Frequency	Rate	Frequency	Rate
Same	28,087	8.9	5,237	0.78	103,333	5.96
Transition	17,090	5.42	13,769	2.05	84,641	4.89
Expansion	58,957	18.68	76,382	11.39	288,725	16.66
Independent	211,449	67	575,425	75.78	1,255,913	72.49

Table 5. Experiment result of Universities based on common patterns

University						
Pattern of invention	U_1		U_2		U_3	
	Frequency	Rate	Frequency	Rate	Frequency	Rate
Same	123,491	0.11	115,615	0.11	113,321	0.12
Transition	468,082	0.43	482,367	0.46	440,320	0.46
Expansion	2,393,747	2.22	2,244,802	2.13	2,209,547	2.3
Independent	105,011,001	97.24	102,777,524	97.31	93,156,171	97.12

Transition (T) patterns. Also, companies have more Same (S) patterns than the research group. In other words, the company focuses on the expansion of existing technologies and the development of related technologies rather than the research institutes. As shown in Table 5, unlike other applicant groups (companies, research institutes), I patterns are the most representative feature of the university. Because universities include different domains, they invent a wide range of technologies rather than focusing on specific domains.

5   Conclusion

Recently, due to the rapid development of technology in the field of information and communication, inventors are making efforts to secure intellectual property rights for new technologies. As a result, the number of patents invented is increasing worldwide. In this environment, studies were carried out to measure the value of technology and to analyze the invention's trends by analyzing the technologies specified in the patent. Various researches extract core technical terms from patents using natural language processing and text mining technology. However, patents are expressed in terms of many new and alternative terms. Therefore the recall rate and the classification accuracy of the patented technology are low. Many studies have been conducted to analyze patents through the proposed CPC. However, existing studies have focused on investigating new technologies or core technologies included in patent documents. As a result, there is still a lack of research to analyze the applicant's value and analyze the inventive trend. In this paper, we propose a model for analyzing the technical inventions of inventors based on the CPC. Through the proposed model, we confirmed that each applicant showed different inventive characteristics by type. Applicants of the company type proved that they invented a new technology based on their technologies. In the case of a university applicant including various domains, it is confirmed that a relatively new pattern of the invention of technology appears in comparison with companies and institutes, Respectively. Besides, the institute showed that it focused on new technology inventions rather than companies. Future studies will collect more patent data of applicants, analyze various cases, and analyze not only Korean patents but also EU and US patents.

References

1. Bongsun, K., Eonsoo, K.: The relationship between patent characteristics and its value: an empirical study in the context of a patent pool. J. Strateg. Manag. 17(3), 163–181 (2014)
2. Yonghyun, K.-Y.: The effects of qualitative patenting activities on firm outcome. In: Proceedings of Spring Conference, pp. 607–610. KIIE: Korean Institute of Industrial Engineers, Korea (2015)
3. Jinho, C., Heesoo, K., Namgyu, I.: Keyword network analysis for technology forecasting. J. Intell. Inf. Syst. 17(4), 227–240 (2011)
4. Sungjun, A.-J.: Business technology trend analysis using patent information. In: Proceedings of Spring Conference, pp. 13–14. KIIS: Korean Institute of Intelligent Systems, Korea (2015)
5. Jongchan, K., Joonhyuck, L., Gabjo, K., Sangsung, P., Dongsik, J.: Data engineering: time series analysis of patent keywords for forecasting emerging technology. KIPS Trans. Softw. Data Eng. 3(9), 355–360 (2014)
6. Jangwon, G., Jinpyo, L., Yunji, J., Doheon, J., Hanmin, J.: A trend analysis method for IoT technologies using patent dataset with goal and approach concepts. Wireless Pers. Commun. 91(4), 1749–1764 (2016)
7. Hyun, W.-J.: Extracting core technology using IPC code analysis and forward citation. In: Proceedings of Spring Conference, pp. 7–8. KIIS: Korean Institute of Intelligent Systems, Korea (2015)

8. Kyoungrae, L.-P.: Technology relation for patent of technology transfer based on IPC code. In: Proceedings of Autumn Conference, pp. 181–182. KIIS: Korean Institute of Intelligent Systems, Korea (2015)
9. Jiho, K., Jongchan, K., Junhyuck, L., Sangsung, P., Dongsik, J.: A patent trend analysis for technological convergence of IoT and wearables. J. Korean Inst. Intell. Syst. **25**(3), 306–311 (2015)

A Study on Automatic Keyphrase Extraction and Its Refinement for Scientific Articles

Yeonsoo Lim, Daehyeon Bong, and Yuchul Jung[✉]

Kumoh National Institute of Technology (KIT), 61 Daehak-ro, Gumi,
Gyeongbuk 39177, South Korea
{yslim6168, jyc}@kumoh.ac.kr,
pkjeogus@naver.com

Abstract. Keyphrase extraction is a fundamental, but very important task in NLP that map documents to a set of representative words/phrases. However, state-of-the-art results on benchmark datasets are still immature stage. As an effort to alleviate the gaps between human annotated keyphrases and automatically extracted ones, in this paper, we introduce our on-going work about how to extract meaningful keyphrases of scientific research articles. Moreover, we investigate several avenues of refining the extracted ones using pre-trained word embeddings and its variations. For the experiments, we use two different datasets (i.e., WWW and KDD) in computer science domain.

Keywords: Keyphrase extraction · Word embedding · Refinement · Scientific articles

1 Introduction

Keyphrases extraction can be defined as "the automatic selection of important and topic phrases from the body of a document" [1, 2]. Especially, the task of keyphrases extraction from scientific articles is of great concerns to researcher and publishers as it helps to recommend articles to users, highlight missing citations to author, analyze research trends overtime, and have a quick overview of the given paper. Due to its widespread use, various studied have been conducted on the automatic extraction of keyphrases using different methods. The main two streams of automatic keyphrases extraction task are unsupervised and supervised.

Unsupervised method for keyphrases extraction are formulated as a ranking problem. Various unsupervised methods has been proposed in the literature can be divided into twos: corpus-dependent and corpus-independent. The key benefits of unsupervised methods over supervised methods is that they doesn't require training data. More recently, some embedding techniques (e.g., word embedding, phrase embedding, and sentence embedding) [3, 4] have been employed to achieve more advanced accuracy. The supervised approaches generally treat the keyphrase extraction as a classification task, in which a learning model is trained on the features of a labelled keyphrases to determine whether a candidate phrase is keyphrase or not. In comparison

© Springer Nature Switzerland AG 2020
M. Brambilla et al. (Eds.): ICWE 2019 Workshops, LNCS 11609, pp. 18–21, 2020.
https://doi.org/10.1007/978-3-030-51253-8_3

with unsupervised methods, most of supervised methods can achieve better results when sufficient training data are given although there are some differences between used algorithms.

However, the keyphrase extraction task is far from solved and the performances of existing approaches are worse in comparison to many other NLP tasks. In this paper, we investigate the possibility of the performance improvements of keyphrase extraction with the use of word embedding and its refinement. To observe the impact of word embeddings, we compare the differences between general-purpose embeddings and domain-specific embeddings.

2 Related Work

In the unsupervised ranking approaches, TF-IDF based ranking has been shown moderate performance in practice. There are several graph based approaches, such as, CiteText-Rank, ExpandRank, SingleRank, TextRank, TopicRank, WordAttraction Rank etc. More recently, [3, 4] integrated information provided by word embedding vectors into a graph-based ranking approach.

Word embeddings that provide continuous low-dimensional vector representations of words have been widely studied by NLP communities. However, the actual distribution obtained from Word2Vec is not normally satisfactory because Word2Vec only focuses on context similarity. To obtain more feasible word embeddings for the given tasks, task-oriented word embeddings for specific task and refinement of pre-trained word embeddings have been studied further. In IR domain, [5] demonstrated that the globally trained word embedding underperform corpus and query-specific embeddings for retrieval tasks. They proposed locally training word embeddings in a query-specific manner for the query expansion task. For sentiment analysis task, [6] refined word embedding to avoid generating similar vector representations for sentimentally opposite words. In case of text classification, a task-oriented word embedding method is suggested to regularize the distribution of word to enable the embedding space to have a clear classification boundary [7].

Our method incorporates multi-version of word embeddings for keyphrase extraction and its refinements to delineate more topical keyphrases from scientific articles.

3 Proposed Methods and Some Findings

Our method consists of the following three key steps:

(1) Candidate extraction: Using YAKE [8], an unsupervised technique, we extract keyphrase candidates automatically. Currently, the unsupervised keyphrase extraction method is the state of the art as of May, 2019.
(2) Re-scoring keyphrase candidates: We compute the scores of candidate keyphrases by applying multiple word embedding strategies (e.g., general-purpose word embeddings and domain-specific word embeddings).

(3) Refinement of the keyphrase candidates: Based on various domain heuristics identified for keyphrase extraction [4], unpromising candidates are filtered out. Finally, we can get the most promising top-k keyphrases for the given abstract.

To evaluate our proposed methods, we use a well-known keyphrase extraction benchmark dataset based on scientific research paper [9]. The datasets contain abstracts from two CS premier conferences: the World Wide Web (WWW) conference and the ACM SIGKDD Conference Knowledge Discovery and Data Mining (KDD). For now, the datasets are available through the github repository (i.e., https://github.com/boudinfl/ake-datasets) and the sizes of them are 1330 (WWW) and 755 (KDD), respectively.

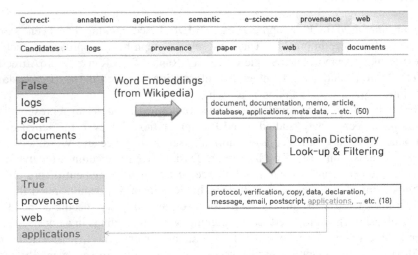

Fig. 1. Modifying general-purpose word embeddings with domain dictionary

Figure 1 shows our basic scheme for using general-purpose word embedding and its refinements. First, we observe the effectiveness of general purpose word embedding based on Wikipedia data. However, simply fetching word embedding from it may fail in suggesting highly-probable candidates for the keyphrase extraction. Second, to see the effectiveness of using domain dictionary (about 3000 entry words), especially computer science domain, the previous obtained 50 words from the general-purpose word embeddings were filtered with the dictionary. We have a firm belief that giving more weights on the remained words in the embedding may contribute to a better accuracy of keyphrase extraction by changing the positions of the high-probable words based on their weights.

Table 1 summarizes the evidences of how many keyphrases can be identified with the help of domain-specific dictionary beyond general-purpose word embeddings in WWW/KDD datasets. It shows that the possibility of accuracy improvements can be increased up to about 2% and 3.7%, respectively.

Table 1. Evidences gotten from WWW/KDD datasets

Dataset	Num. of incorrect KPs	Num. of correctable KPs
KDD	1545	32 (2.07%)
WWW	1464	54 (3.69%)

4   Concluding Remarks

In this paper, we outlined our on-going work for advanced unsupervised keyphrase extraction from scientific articles. Our approaches are quite empirical, thus the preliminary results may be far from state of the art accuracy. Use of various types of external resources, such as Wikipedia data (science & technology only) and arXiv.org for the refinement of pre-trained word embeddings and sophisticated re-ranking algorithms will be studied further as future work.

References

1. Wan, X., Xiao, J.: Single document keyphrase extraction using neighborhood knowledge. In: Proceedings of the 23rd National Conference on Artificial Intelligence, pp. 855–860 (2008)
2. Mothe, J., Rasolomanana, M.: Automatic keyphrase extraction using graph-based methods. In: Proceedings of the 33rd Annual ACM Symposium on Applied Computing, pp. 728–730 (2018)
3. Bennani-Smires, K., Musat, C., Hossmann, A., Baeriswyl, M., Jaggi, M.: Simple unsupervised keyphrase extraction using sentence embeddings. In: Proceedings of the 22nd Conference on Computational Natural Language Learning (CoNLL), pp. 221–229 (2018)
4. Mahata, D., Kuriakose, J., Shah, R.R., Zimmermann, R.: Key2Vec: automatic ranked keyphrase extraction from scientific articles using phrase embeddings. In: Proceedings of the 2018 Conference of the North American Chapter of the Association for Computational Linguistics: Human Language Technologies, pp. 634–639 (2018)
5. Diaz, F., Mitra, B., Craswell, N.: Query expansion with locally-trained word embeddings. In: Proceedings of the 54th Annual Meeting of the Association for Computational Linguistics, pp. 367–377 (2016)
6. Yu, L.-C., Wang, J., Lai, K.R., Zhang, X.: Refining word embeddings for sentiment analysis. In: Proceedings of the 2017 Conference on Empirical Methods in Natural Language Processing, pp. 534–539 (2017)
7. Liu, Q., Huang, H., Gao, Y., Wei, X., Tian, Y., Liu, L.: Task-oriented word embedding for text classification. In: Proceedings of the 27th International Conference on Computational Linguistics, pp. 2023–2032 (2018)
8. Campos, R., Mangaravite, V., Pasquali, A., Jorge, A.M., Nunes, C., Jatowt, A.: YAKE! collection-independent automatic keyword extractor. In: Pasi, G., Piwowarski, B., Azzopardi, L., Hanbury, A. (eds.) ECIR 2018. LNCS, vol. 10772, pp. 806–810. Springer, Cham (2018). https://doi.org/10.1007/978-3-319-76941-7_80
9. Caragea, C., Bulgarov, F.A., Godea, A., Das Gollapalli, S.: Citation-enhanced keyphrase extraction from research papers: a supervised approach. In: Proceedings of the 2014 Conference on Empirical Methods in Natural Language Processing, pp. 1435–1446 (2014)

A Study on the Characteristics of the Long-Term Web Forum Users Using Social Network Analysis

Min Jung Lee[1] and Jiyoung Woo[2(✉)]

[1] Sejong Cyber University, 121, Gunja-ro, Gwangjin-gu,
Seoul, Republic of Korea
mjlee@sjcu.ac.kr
[2] Soonchunhyang University, 22, Soonchunhyang-ro, Sinchang-myeon,
Asan-si, Chungcheongnam-do, Republic of Korea
jy0503.woo@gmail.com

Abstract. A web forum is an online place where people who are interested in a specific topic talk with each other. A medical web forum has been used to obtain the health and wellbeing information to prepare for an aging society. This paper proposes the methodology using sentiment analysis and social network analysis to identify the factors which turn newbies into long-term users in the medical web forum. In particular, this study analyzes the influences of the social network of the Alzheimer's Disease & Dementia (AD) medical web forum and suggests strategies to help patients, their family and medical officials suffering from Alzheimer.

Keywords: Web forum · Social network · Long-term users

1 Introduction

The development of ICT (information and communications technology) has a major impact on the medical field [1]. Long-term medical treatment became necessary as human life span was extended through new drug development, incurable disease treatment, and disease prevention. 59% of adults use online contents to find new health information, and 34% of health searchers use social media such as medical web forum to obtain the knowledge from experiences [2].

In 2017, 121,404 people died from AD (Alzheimer's Disease & Dementia) which is the sixth leading cause of death in US. Deaths due to stroke, heart disease reduced, whereas deaths due to AD increased 145%. AD causes mental impact such as emotional distress and negative mental and enormous costs to patients as well as their family [3]. The advantages of medical web form are follows [4]: Patients and their families can receive information support (e.g., remedies, medical technologies, healthcare) and emotion support (e.g., sympathy, and empathy) [5]. As patients suffering from the incurable disease in the age of aging increase and the long-term care is needed, the use of medical web forums is continuously growing for information and emotion supports [6, 7].

M. Brambilla et al. (Eds.): ICWE 2019 Workshops, LNCS 11609, pp. 22–26, 2020.
https://doi.org/10.1007/978-3-030-51253-8_4

The Healthborad.com [8] which is also one of the largest and most dynamic on the Web, with over 10 million monthly visitors, 850,000 registered members, and over 4.5 million messages posted. HealthBoards was rated as one of the top 20 health information websites by Consumer Reports Health WebWatch. Especially, we used the Alzheimer's Disease & Dementia category among many discussion boards within it, which is a major community within the Healthborad.com. Recently, the usage of AD web forum has decreased, including the number of posts, user access and views.

The purpose of this study is to suggest a method to reactivate the web forum by deriving the factors through analysis of long-term user's usage pattern and social network structure. The following research questions will be addressed:

1. Are the thread patterns which users post in the medical web forum are related to long-term use?
2. Do the thread patterns during initial 2 months affect how users embed in social network measures among the users?
3. Are the sentimental analysis measures (ratio of positive/negative words, number of positive/negative words) related to the social network measures (degree centrality, betweenness centrality, closeness centrality, Bonacich Power) among the users?

2 Methodology

We set our experiment arena to online health web forum, where people exchange information in common people's language and provide emotional supports to patients and their related ones. We chose the Alzheimer's Disease & Dementia discussion boards from among the many discussion boards in the Healthborad.com.

We developed an integrated crawler and parser to collect data from the web forum.

The parser extract data fields such as the thread ID, message ID, author ID, posting time, and message. The parsed fields were stored in a database.

8,025 articles were extracted from the bulletin board including 158 threads and 7,867 comments for 5 years. We found that 261 users participated in discussion in the web forum and 123 users remained except those who participated once or twice.

The threads are classified into the starter thread and threads depending on whether you posted the starter thread. Then users of the medical web forum are classified into the data during the initial two months of each user and the data during 5 years (Fig. 1).

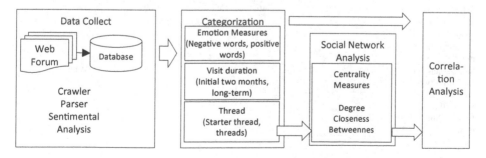

Fig. 1. A process of data analysis from the medical web forum

First, we performed data preprocessing. We converted text to lowercase and removed punctuations, numbers, and stopwords. Stopwords have no special meaning, but are frequently used such as, "a", "the" and "is". Then, we performed tokenizing and stemming to derive basic words.

We then performed the sentiment analysis results using General Inquirer using Harvard IV-4 TagNeg (H4N) dictionary after crawling and parsing data. Each word is checked whether it is positive or negative through the dictionary in the general inquirer. Each posting is calculated in terms of the positive words and negative words.

We aggregated message-level features to author-level by calculating the positive rate as ratio of the positive words over the total words and the negative rate as ratio of the negative words over the total words. The emotion rate is calculated as the sum of positive words and negative words over the total words. The information rate is the difference of 1 and the emotion rate.

The social network is constructed reflecting the relationship between thread and replies. The centrality measures are calculated by social network analysis. Applying each step of the experimental procedure, we obtained the data regarding the behavior pattern in web forum, the centrality measures and emotion measures, allowing performing the correlation analysis.

3   Evaluation and Conclusion

To test the relation between the usage periods of web forum and the thread patterns, a Spearman correlation was applied using SPSS. Table 1 gives an overview of the correlations between the long-term use, namely users' life time and posting patterns. The posting patterns is categorized the threads, self-threads, starter thread. The starter thread refers opening a thread. Self-thread refers that the author leaves replies to own starter thread. The threads include starter-threads and replies. We count the user's life time as the number of months that the user participating in threading.

Table 1. Correlations between characteristics of behavior patterns (N = 123)

	Life time	Threads	Self-threads	Starter threads	Threads for the initial two months	Self-threads for the initial two months	Starter-threads for the initial two months
Life time	1	.421(**)	.698(**)	.411(**)	.429(**)	-0.054	0.013
Threads		1	.605(**)	.951(**)	.865(**)	.323(**)	.289(**)
Self-threads			1	.546(**)	.559(**)	0.009	.204(*)
Starter thread				1	.795(**)	.384(**)	.241(**)
Threads during the initial two months				.	1	.244(**)	.321(**)
Self-threads for the initial two months						1	.540(**)
Starter-threads for the initial two months							1

The correlation between the users' life time and the number of posting threading for the initial 2 months is significant moderate with the value of 0.429. The life time is strongly related to self-treads and moderately related to the number of threads and starter treads.

The results for the correlation between posting behaviors and the SNA measures of degree centrality, betweenness centrality, closeness centrality, bonacich power are presented in Table 2. Overall, the posting patterns naturally affect the centrality of users within the social network. But interestingly, the initial patterns for two months decide the centrality of users within the social network.

In more details, the closeness centrality was not statistically significantly related to the life time, 'self-threads' and 'starter-threads for the first 2 months'. Those results imply that as those groups were not key groups in the network or didn't have important information. The betweenness centrality was not statistically significantly related to 'Self-threads for the initial 2 months'. This shows the users who replied multiple times on their own starter thread could not move on to the role of mediator in the social network.

The sentiment analysis on threads shows that the number of sent-words whether they are positive and negative affect to user's centrality within the social network.

Table 2. Correlation between social network analysis measures and behavior (N = 123).

Posting behaviors	Degree centrality	Closeness centrality	Betweenness centrality	Bonacich power
Life time	.440(**)	−0.002	.403(**)	.289(**)
Threads	.890(**)	.273(**)	.543(**)	.944(**)
Self-threads	.809(**)	0.038	.573(**)	.541(**)
Starter threads	.823(**)	.272(**)	.505(**)	.885(**)
Threads for the initial 2 months*	**.727(**)**	**.252(**)**	**.425(**)**	**.712(**)**
Self-threads for the initial 2 months	.188(*)	.231(*)	**0.095**	.321(**)
Starter threads for the initial 2 months	.278(**)	0.02	.263(**)	.258(**)
Use ratio of positive words	0.08	−0.092	0.16	0.044
Use ratio of negative words	0.047	−0.106	0.072	0.005
Use ratio of information words	−0.092	0.135	−0.172	−0.039
Number of positive words	.950(**)	0.125	.583(**)	.806(**)
Number of negative words	.955(**)	0.108	.567(**)	.806(**)

In order to identify the factors which are related to long-term usages, posting pattern and social network measures in the medical web forum, this study proposed a method using sentimental analysis, the social network analysis. The users for the initial 2 months are classified into 3 groups: (1) the first group who posts threads has the significant correlation of all the 4 centrality measures, (2) the second group who posts reply-threads to his own thread has the non-significant correlation of betweenness centrality which means that nodes act as 'bridges' between nodes in a network, (3) the last group who raise issues thread has the non-significant correlation of closeness centrality which means the individuals who are placed to influence the entire network.

Further research is needed to investigate the causes and effect of the decrease of AD medical web forum usages and formulate the general strategies for activating it.

References

1. Elkin, N.: How America searches: health and wellness, iCrossing (2008)
2. Alzheimer's Association: Alzheimer's disease facts and figures. Alzheimer's Dement. **15**, 321–387 (2019)
3. Woo, J., et al.: Modeling the dynamics of medical information through web forums in medical industry. Technol. Forecast. Soc. Chang. **97**, 77–90 (2015)
4. Lee, M., et al.: The analysis on users' centrality in the social network and their sentiment: applying to medical web forum on Alzheimer's Disease. J. Korea Soc. Comput. Inf. **20**(6), 127–140 (2015)
5. Wicks, P., et al.: Perceived benefits of sharing health data between people with epilepsy on an online platform. Epilepsy Behav. **23**, 16–23 (2012)
6. Lee, Y., et al.: Long-term care facilities: important participants of the acute care facility social network? PLoS ONE **6**(12), e29342 (2011)
7. The Healthborad. https://www.healthboards.com. Accessed 19 May 2019

Knowledge Exploration from Tables on the Web

Haklae Kim$^{(\boxtimes)}$

Chung-Ang University, 84 Heukseok-ro, Dongjak-gu, Seoul, Korea
haklaekim@cau.ac.kr

Abstract. Tables in Web pages are the main source of knowledge graphs because they contain summarised information. Since there are various ways to represent information in web tables, it is not easy to extract information efficiently. This paper proposes a method for extracting information from structured and unstructured web pages and a method for converting the extracted information into a knowledge graph. In particular, in order to construct a Korean knowledge graph, this paper introduces a method for extracting large table data from web pages that are written in Korean and expressing it in a graph.

Keywords: Tabular data · Knowledge graph · Knowledge extraction · Knowledge creation

1 Introduction

The importance of a knowledge base is emphasised as a rapid expansion of artificial intelligence services. A knowledge base represents semantic information about entities and their relationships. A number of knowledge base has developed with their own purposes such as Google's Knowledge Graph [7], DBpedia [1], Wikidata [6], or Freebase [2], etc. Existing knowledge bases, however, do not develop from the scratch. When it comes to develop a knowledge base, it is common for extracting factual knowledge from various data sources such as Wikipedia or web documents.

Some studies provide a knowledge extraction framework from a web table [3]. Munoz et al. [5] introduce DRETa to extract RDF triples from generic Wikipedia tables. This tool matches entities in table cells to entities in a reference knowledge base to look for potential relations that hold between entities on the same row across two given columns. However, DRETa is only served for Wikipedia tables and strongly relies on DBpedia. Limaye et al. [4] propose a machine learning techniques to annotate table cells with entity, type and relation information. They associates one or more types with each column of the table, annotates pairs of columns with a binary relation in the catalog and annotates table cells with entity IDs in the catalog, when it is believed that the cell makes a reference to the entity. It focuses on table annotation regardless of detecting tables from a web document. On the other hand, there are some studies that extract and

© Springer Nature Switzerland AG 2020
M. Brambilla et al. (Eds.): ICWE 2019 Workshops, LNCS 11609, pp. 27–30, 2020.
https://doi.org/10.1007/978-3-030-51253-8_5

update a knowledge base from a web table. [8] proposes a method for building a knowledge base using linguistic patterns to extract a probabilistic taxonomy of classes and entities from web texts, and then create factual knowledge about the attributes of the entities using web tables. This paper introduces a novel method to efficiently extract knowledge from a web table. To effectively extract knowledge from tables, the proposed method evaluates the quality of the table and reduces the scope of knowledge extraction before extracting knowledge from the table. The reminder of this paper is organised as follows. Section 2 introduces a concept of constructing knowledge from web tables with the proposed model. Section 3 describes the evaluation of the proposed approach by using datasets that are collected on the Web. And Sect. 4 concludes and outlines the plans for future research.

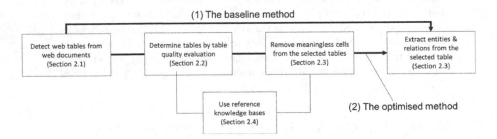

Fig. 1. A process of knowledge extraction from a web table

2   Knowledge Acquisition from a Web Table

A web table contains relational or structured data describing a set of entities. In general, acquiring knowledge from web tables comprises of three steps: (1) detecting a table from a web document, (2) extracting factual knowledge from the web table and (3) transforming the facts to a knowledge base. Each step can improve performance through a variety of approaches. One of issues to extracting knowledge from a web table is quality of extracted information. Note that meaningless information such as an empty value might be included in a web table, it would be the reason of increasing the inefficiency of knowledge extraction and construction. This paper focuses on determining potential candidates by evaluating the quality of a table for extracting meaningful information from the table. As shown in Fig. 1, the *baseline* method detects a relational table and extracts the information of the detected table without loss of information, whereas the *optimised* method reflects table quality for determining tables for knowledge extraction. The optimised one evaluates the quality of the data contained in the table, and eliminates the incomplete information to specify the object of knowledge extraction. The following addresses details of each process by expanding a proposed method.

2.1 Table Detection

A table as web content is represented by various formats with different tag styles. For example, the <table> tag defines an HTML table, it consists of one or more <tr>, <th>, and <td> elements. The <ul> and <li> tag can be used to represent a table, although <ul> tag together with the <li> defines to create lists. On the other hand, some websites uses their own HTML tags for representing a table. For example, Wikipedia employs the <wikitable> tag, which is a box of rows and columns used to describe data.

Thus, it is important to recognise different types of embedment to extract tables from web documents. To better detect tables, an improved approach based the work [9] is extended. A set of rules is predefined for detecting a web table and for extracting an value of each cell from the detected table. For example, this rule (//div[@id = 'main']/table[1]/tbody/tr[1]/th[1]) by using XPath is used to extract one of values in a web table. 'tr[1]' defines first row and 'th[1]' defines first column. Note that decision tree is used to learn predefined rules to obtain the relational table classifier.

2.2 Reference Knowledge Base

For extracting knowledge from a web table, existing knowledge bases play an important role to annotate cells and its relations. Freebase and Wikidata are used for a reference knowledge in this purpose. Freebase is a large collaborative knowledge base consisting of metadata composed mainly by its community members [2]. Wikidata is a free, collaborative, multilingual, secondary database, collecting structured data to provide support for Wikipedia [6]. Since both knowledge bases contain considerable knowledge facts (i.e. Freebase: about 1.35B triples, Wikidata: 0.6B triples), both KBs are indexed for executing large amount of retrievals in the process of evaluating table quality and table annotation. Note that the structure of indexed knowledge is refactored to support fast candidate entity retrieval based on Apache Lucene, although knowledge facts from both KBs are represented as a triple format.

3 Evaluation

To evaluate the proposed method, a set of web documents are collected, and then each evaluation is carried out. All tests are carried out on local Linux PC (i7-7700K CPU and 32G memory). First, it is essential to evaluate the performance of the pre-defined rules for table detection. In this purpose, 2,930 HTML pages from around 150 websites are aggregated. By testing and updating the predefined rules, F-measure of the table detection reaches 96.74% and precision 98.32%.

In order to evaluate performance of table quality and table annotation, 102,348 web documents about culture, history, sports and politics were collected and 24,358 tables were extracted. The average number of rows and columns in the extracted table is 15.7 and 9.3, respectively. The maximum number of rows and columns in a table is 1670 and 145, respectively.

4   Conclusions

This paper introduces a novel method to efficiently extract knowledge from a web table. A web table is a way to represent data structurally, but there are a number of issues with recognising tables contained in a web document and transforming the data contained in the table into a knowledge base. Extracting the data contained in a table from a large Web document requires a lot of effort. This paper evaluates the quality of a table before extracting knowledge from the table. The information contained in the table is used to determine whether to extract knowledge by calculating completeness and accuracy. In addition, a method to remove meaningless information from a table is proposed to reduce the scope of knowledge extraction.

This paper does not include the process of adding entities and their relationships extracted from a table to a knowledge base. Future studies include improving the accuracy of extracted information to add or update information extracted from tables into the knowledge base.

References

1. Auer, S., Bizer, C., Kobilarov, G., Lehmann, J., Cyganiak, R., Ives, Z.: DBpedia: a nucleus for a web of open data. In: Aberer, K., et al. (eds.) ASWC/ISWC -2007. LNCS, vol. 4825, pp. 722–735. Springer, Heidelberg (2007). https://doi.org/10.1007/978-3-540-76298-0_52
2. Bollacker, K., Evans, C., Paritosh, P., Sturge, T., Taylor, J.: Freebase: a collaboratively created graph database for structuring human knowledge. In: Proceedings of the 2008 ACM SIGMOD International Conference on Management of Data, SIGMOD 2008, pp. 1247–1250. ACM, New York (2008)
3. Kim, H., He, L., Di, Y.: Knowledge extraction framework for building a largescale knowledge base. EAI Endorsed Trans. Ind. Netw. Intell. Syst. 3(7), e2 (2016)
4. Limaye, G., Sarawagi, S., Chakrabarti, S.: Annotating and searching web tables using entities, types and relationships. PVLDB 3(1), 1338–1347 (2010)
5. Muñoz, E., Hogan, A., Mileo, A.: DRETa: extracting RDF from wikitables. In: Blomqvist, E., Groza, T. (eds.) International Semantic Web Conference (Posters and Demos). CEUR Workshop Proceedings, vol. 1035, pp. 89–92. CEUR-WS.org (2013)
6. Pellissier Tanon, T., Vrandečić, D., Schaffert, S., Steiner, T., Pintscher, L.: From freebase to Wikidata: the great migration. In: Proceedings of the 25th International Conference on World Wide Web, WWW 2016, pp. 1419–1428. International World Wide Web Conferences Steering Committee, Republic and Canton of Geneva (2016)
7. Singhal, A.: Introducing the knowledge graph: things, not strings (2012). https://www.blog.google/products/search/introducing-knowledge-graph-things-not/
8. Wang, J., Wang, H., Wang, Z., Zhu, K.Q.: Understanding tables on the web. In: Atzeni, P., Cheung, D., Ram, S. (eds.) ER 2012. LNCS, vol. 7532, pp. 141–155. Springer, Heidelberg (2012). https://doi.org/10.1007/978-3-642-34002-4_11
9. Wang, Y., Hu, J.: A machine learning based approach for table detection on the web. In: Lassner, D., Roure, D.D., Iyengar, A. (eds.) WWW, pp. 242–250. ACM (2002)

5th International Workshop on Knowledge Discovery on the Web (KDWEB 2019)

5th International Workshop on Knowledge Discovery on the Web (KDWEB 2019)

The fifth edition of the international workshop on Knowledge Discovery on the Web has been a satellite event of the International Conference on Web Engineering for the second time after the first successful coordination of the event in 2018.

We have had nine submissions, among which we accepted four papers. The accepted papers range among different aspects of machine learning and other issues of Knowledge Discovery in web engineering. The first paper, by Tomonari Masada, titled *Context-dependent Token-wise Variational Autoencoder for Topic Modeling* explores the problem of autocoding topic modeling, an issue that is central in online documental systems. The second paper, instead, looks at the discovery of relations that result from interactions in social network, being a combination of the approaches in Statistical Natural Language Processing with the approaches in link analysis and mining. The paper is authored by Marco Adriani, Marco Brambilla and Marco Di Giovanni and titled *Extraction of Relations between Entities from Human-Generated Content on Social Networks*. The third paper, *Social networks as communication channels: a logical approach* discusses a theoretical model of the communication channels and provides a framework to interpret communication actions. Authors are Matteo Cristani, Francesco Olivieri and Katia Santacà. By Matteo Cristani and Claudio Tomazzoli, we have the last paper: *Dataset anonymization on cloud: open problems and perspectives*, that presents a technical review of the open problems in dataset anonymization.

The quality of the presented papers and their value is neat, and the overall discussion provided by the authors within the workshop has shown the importance of the theme in the community of Web Engineering.

June 2019

Giuliano Armano
Matteo Cristani

KDWEB 2019 Organization

Workshop Chairs

Giuliano Armano   Department of Electrical and Electronic Engineering,
                           University of Cagliari, Italy
Matteo Cristani   Department of Computer Science – University of Verona, Italy

Publication Chair

Alessandro Giuliani   Department of Electrical and Electronic Engineering –
                        University of Cagliari, Italy

Publicity Chair

Claudio Tomazzoli   Department of Computer Science, University of Verona, Italy

Context-Dependent Token-Wise Variational Autoencoder for Topic Modeling

Tomonari Masada$^{(\boxtimes)}$ (iD)

Nagasaki University,1-14 Bunkyo-machi, Nagasaki-shi, Nagasaki, Japan
masada@nagasaki-u.ac.jp

Abstract. This paper proposes a new variational autoencoder (VAE) for topic models. The variational inference (VI) for Bayesian models approximates the true posterior distribution by maximizing a lower bound of the log marginal likelihood of observations. We can implement VI as VAE by using a neural network called encoder to obtain parameters of approximate posterior. Our contribution is three-fold. First, we marginalize out per-document topic probabilities by following the proposal by Mimno et al. This marginalizing out has not been considered in the existing VAE proposals for topic modeling to the best of our knowledge. Second, after marginalizing out topic probabilities, we need to approximate the posterior probabilities of token-wise topic assignments. However, this posterior is categorical and thus cannot be approximated by continuous distributions like Gaussian. Therefore, we adopt the Gumbel-softmax trick. Third, while we can sample token-wise topic assignments with the Gumbel-softmax trick, we should consider document-wide contextual information for a better approximation. Therefore, we feed to our encoder network a concatenation of token-wise information and document-wide information, where the former is implemented as word embedding and the latter as the document-wide mean of word embeddings. The experimental results showed that our VAE improved the existing VAE proposals for a half of the data sets in terms of perplexity or of normalized pairwise mutual information (NPMI).

Keywords: Topic modeling · Deep learning · Variational autoencoder

1 Introduction

Topic modeling is a well-known text analysis method adopted not only in Web data mining but also in a wide variety of research disciplines, including social sciences[1] and digital humanities.[2] Topic modeling extracts *topics* from a large

---

[1] https://www.structuraltopicmodel.com/.
[2] https://www.gale.com/intl/primary-sources/digital-scholar-lab.

© Springer Nature Switzerland AG 2020
M. Brambilla et al. (Eds.): ICWE 2019 Workshops, LNCS 11609, pp. 35–47, 2020.
https://doi.org/10.1007/978-3-030-51253-8_6

document set, where topics are defined as categorical distribution over vocabulary words. Each topic is expected to put high probabilities on the words expressing one among the clear-cut semantic contents delivered by the document set. For example, the news articles talking about science may use the words that are rarely used by the articles talking about politics, and vice versa. Topic modeling can explicate such a difference by providing two different word categorical distributions, one putting high probabilities on the words like experiment, hypothesis, laboratory, etc, and another on the words like government, vote, parliament, etc. Topic modeling achieves two things at the same time. First, it provides topics as categorical distributions defined over words as stated above. Second, it also provides topic probabilities for each document. Topic probabilities are expected to be effective as a lower-dimensional representation of documents, which reflects the difference of their semantic contents.

This paper discusses the inference for Bayesian topic models. The inference aims to approximate the posterior distribution. The sampling-based approaches like MCMC approximate the posterior by drawing samples from it. While samples are drawn from the true posterior, we can only access the posterior through the drawn samples. This paper focuses on the variational inference (VI), which approximates the posterior with a tractable surrogate distribution. Our task in VI is to estimate the parameters of the surrogate distribution. VI maximizes a lower bound of the log marginal likelihood $\log p(\mathbf{x}_d)$ for every document $\mathbf{x}_d$. The lower bound is obtained by applying Jensen's inequality as follows:

$$
\log p(\mathbf{x}_d) = \log \int p(\mathbf{x}_d|\mathbf{\Phi})p(\mathbf{\Phi})d\mathbf{\Phi} = \log \int q(\mathbf{\Phi})\frac{p(\mathbf{x}_d|\mathbf{\Phi})p(\mathbf{\Phi})}{q(\mathbf{\Phi})}d\mathbf{\Phi}
$$

$$
\geq \int q(\mathbf{\Phi})\log \frac{p(\mathbf{x}_d|\mathbf{\Phi})p(\mathbf{\Phi})}{q(\mathbf{\Phi})}d\mathbf{\Phi} = \mathbb{E}_{q(\mathbf{\Phi})}\big[\log p(\mathbf{x}_d|\mathbf{\Phi})\big] - \mathrm{KL}(q(\mathbf{\Phi}) \parallel p(\mathbf{\Phi})) \equiv \mathcal{L}_d
$$

$$(1)$$

where $\mathbf{\Phi}$ are the model parameters and $q(\mathbf{\Phi})$ a surrogate distribution approximating the true posterior. This lower bound is often called ELBO (Evidence Lower BOund), which we denote by $\mathcal{L}_d$. The maximization of $\mathcal{L}_d$ makes $q(\mathbf{\Phi})$ an approximation of the true posterior $p(\mathbf{\Phi}|\mathbf{x}_d)$.

In this paper, we consider the variational autoencoder (VAE) [10], a variational inference using a neural network for approximating the true posterior. To estimate the parameters of the approximate posterior $q(\mathbf{\Phi})$ in Eq. (1), we can use a neural network called *encoder* as follows. By feeding each observed document $\mathbf{x}_d$ as an input to the encoder, we obtain the parameters of the document-dependent approximate posterior $q(\mathbf{\Phi}|\mathbf{x}_d)$ as the corresponding output. Since the weights and biases of the encoder network is shared by all documents, the inference is performed in an amortized manner. Further, we approximate the ELBO in Eq. (1) by using Monte Carlo integration:

$$
\mathcal{L}_d \approx \frac{1}{S}\sum_{s=1}^{S}\log p(\mathbf{x}_d|\hat{\mathbf{\Phi}}^{(s)}) - \frac{1}{S}\sum_{s=1}^{S}\log q(\hat{\mathbf{\Phi}}^{(s)}|\mathbf{x}_d) - \log p(\hat{\mathbf{\Phi}}^{(s)}) \qquad (2)
$$

where $\hat{\mathbf{\Phi}}^{(s)}$ are the samples drawn from $q(\mathbf{\Phi}|\mathbf{x}_d)$. The sampling $\hat{\mathbf{\Phi}} \sim q(\mathbf{\Phi}|\mathbf{x}_d)$ can be performed by using reparameterization trick [10,18,20,24]. For example, if we choose approximate posteriors from among the multivariate diagonal Gaussian distributions $\mathcal{N}(\boldsymbol{\mu}(\mathbf{x}_d), \boldsymbol{\sigma}(\mathbf{x}_d))$ of dimension K, we use an encoder with $2K$ outputs, the one half of which are used as mean parameters $\boldsymbol{\mu}(\cdot)$ and the other half as log standard deviation parameters $\log \boldsymbol{\sigma}(\cdot)$. We then obtain a sample $\hat{\mathbf{\Phi}} \sim \mathcal{N}(\boldsymbol{\mu}(\mathbf{x}_d), \boldsymbol{\sigma}(\mathbf{x}_d))$ by using a sample $\hat{\boldsymbol{\epsilon}}$ from the K-dimensional standard Gaussian distribution as $\hat{\mathbf{\Phi}} = \hat{\boldsymbol{\epsilon}} \odot \boldsymbol{\sigma}(\mathbf{x}_d) + \boldsymbol{\mu}(\mathbf{x}_d)$, where $\odot$ is the element-wise multiplication. The reparameterization trick enables us to backpropagate to the weights and biases defining the encoder network through samples. While $\mathcal{L}_d$ in Eq. (2) is formulated for a particular document $\mathbf{x}_d$, we maximize the ELBO for many documents simultaneously by using mini-batch optimization.

In this paper, we propose a new VAE for topic modeling. Our contribution is three-fold. *First*, we marginalize out per-document topic probabilities by following the proposal of Mimno et al. [15]. This marginalizing out has not been considered in the existing VAE proposals for topic modeling [3,13,22,26] to the best of our knowledge. *Second*, after marginalizing out topic probabilities, we need to approximate the posterior probabilities of token-wise topic assignments. However, this posterior is categorical and thus cannot be approximated by continuous distributions like Gaussian. Therefore, we draw the approximate posterior samples by using the Gumbel-softmax trick [7]. *Third*, while we can sample a topic assignment for each word token with the Gumbel-softmax trick, we should consider document-wide contextual information for a better approximation. Therefore, we make the input of our encoder a concatenation of token-wise information and document-wide information. We implement the former as word embedding and the latter as the document-wide average of the word embeddings. While we only consider latent Dirichlet allocation (LDA) [1], a similar proposal can be given also for other topic models. The evaluation experiment was conducted over four large document sets. The results showed that the proposed VAE improved the previous VAE proposals for a half of the data sets in terms of perplexity or of normalized pairwise mutual information (NPMI).

The rest of the paper is organized as follows. Section 2 introduces LDA and describes the details of our proposal. Section 3 gives the results of the experiment where we compare our new VAE with other variational inference methods for LDA. Section 4 discusses relevant previous work. Section 5 concludes the paper by suggesting future research directions.

2   Method

2.1   Latent Dirichlet Allocation (LDA)

This subsection introduces LDA [1], for which we propose a new VAE. Assume that there are D documents $\mathbf{X} = \{\mathbf{x}_1, \ldots, \mathbf{x}_D\}$. We denote the vocabulary size by V and the vocabulary set by $\{w_1, \ldots, w_V\}$. Each document $\mathbf{x}_d$ is represented as bag-of-words, i.e., as a multiset of words. The total number of the word tokens in $\mathbf{x}_d$ is referred to by n_d. Let $x_{d,i}$ be the observable random variable giving the index of the word appearing as the i-th token in $\mathbf{x}_d$. That is, $x_{d,i} = v$ means that a token of the word w_v appears as the i-th token in $\mathbf{x}_d$. Topic modeling assigns each word token to one among the fixed number of topics. This can be regarded as a token-level clustering. We denote the number of topics by K and the topic set by $\{t_1, \ldots, t_K\}$. Let $z_{d,i}$ be the latent random variable giving the index of the topic to which $x_{d,i}$ is assigned. That is, $z_{d,i} = k$ means that the i-th word token in $\mathbf{x}_d$ is assigned to the topic t_k.

LDA is a generative model, which generates the data set $\mathbf{X}$ as below. First of all, we assume that a categorical distribution $\text{Categorical}(\boldsymbol{\beta}_k)$ is prepared for each topic t_k, where $\beta_{k,v}$ is the probability of the word w_v in the topic t_k. $\boldsymbol{\beta}_k = (\beta_{k,1}, \ldots, \beta_{k,V})$ satisfies $\sum_v \beta_{k,v} = 1$. LDA generates documents as follows:

– For $d = 1, \ldots, D$:
  • A parameter vector $\boldsymbol{\theta}_d = (\theta_{d,1}, \ldots, \theta_{d,K})$ of the categorical distribution $\text{Categorical}(\boldsymbol{\theta}_d)$ is drawn from the symmetric Dirichlet prior $\text{Dirichlet}(\alpha)$.
  • For $i = 1, \ldots, n_d$:
    * A latent topic $z_{d,i}$ is drawn from $\text{Categorical}(\boldsymbol{\theta}_d)$
    * A word $x_{d,i}$ is drawn from $\text{Categorical}(\boldsymbol{\beta}_{z_{d,i}})$.

where $\theta_{d,k}$ is the probability of the topic t_k in $\mathbf{x}_d$. In this paper, we apply no prior distribution to the categorical distributions $\text{Categorical}(\boldsymbol{\beta}_k)$ for $k = 1, \ldots, K$.

Based on the above generative story, the marginal likelihood (also termed the evidence) of each document $\mathbf{x}_d$ for $d = 1, \ldots, D$ can be given as follows:

$$p(\mathbf{x}_d; \alpha, \boldsymbol{\beta}) = \int \left(\sum_{\mathbf{z}_d} p(\mathbf{x}_d | \mathbf{z}_d; \boldsymbol{\beta}) p(\mathbf{z}_d | \boldsymbol{\theta}_d) \right) p(\boldsymbol{\theta}_d; \alpha) d\boldsymbol{\theta}_d \qquad (3)$$

where $p(\boldsymbol{\theta}_d; \alpha)$ represents the prior $\text{Dirichlet}(\alpha)$. The variational inference (VI) given in [1] maximizes the following lower bound of the log evidence:

$$\log p(\mathbf{x}_d; \alpha, \boldsymbol{\beta}) \geq \mathbb{E}_{q(\mathbf{z}_d)} \left[\log p(\mathbf{x}_d | \mathbf{z}_d; \boldsymbol{\beta}) \right] + \mathbb{E}_{q(\boldsymbol{\theta}_d) q(\mathbf{z}_d)} \left[\log p(\mathbf{z}_d | \boldsymbol{\theta}_d) \right]$$
$$- \text{KL}(q(\boldsymbol{\theta}_d) \, \| \, p(\boldsymbol{\theta}_d; \alpha)) - \mathbb{E}_{q(\mathbf{z}_d)} \left[\log q(\mathbf{z}_d) \right] \qquad (4)$$

This lower bound is obtained by applying Jensen's inequality as in Eq. (1) and is often called ELBO (Evidence Lower BOund).

In the VI proposed by [1], the variational distribution $q(\boldsymbol{\theta}_d)$ is a Dirichlet distribution parameterized separately for each document. That is, there is no direct connections between the variational parameters of different documents. Variational autoencoders (VAEs) for topic modeling [14,22] replace the variational posterior parameterized in a document-wise manner with an amortized variational posterior $q(\boldsymbol{\theta}_d | \mathbf{x}_d)$ by using a neural network whose weights and biases are shared by all documents. However, the existing VAEs for LDA marginalize out the discrete variables $z_{d,i}$ representing topic assignments of word tokens. In this paper, we propose a new VAE, which does not marginalize out the $z_{d,i}$'s. The experimental results will show that our VAE can achieve an effective posterior inference for LDA, which is comparable with the existing VAEs in terms of perplexity or of normalized pairwise mutual information (NPMI). That is, our proposal can be used as an alternative to the previous ones.

2.2 Context-Dependent and Token-Wise VAE for LDA

In this paper, we follow Mimno et al. [15] and marginalize out per-document topic probabilities $\boldsymbol{\theta}_d$ in Eq. (3). We then obtain the following evidence:

$$p(\mathbf{x}_d; \alpha, \boldsymbol{\beta}) = \sum_{\mathbf{z}_d} p(\mathbf{x}_d|\mathbf{z}_d; \boldsymbol{\beta})p(\mathbf{z}_d; \alpha) \tag{5}$$

After marginalizing out $\boldsymbol{\theta}_d$ in this manner, we need to approximate the posterior over the topic assignments $\mathbf{z}_d$. The ELBO to be maximized in our case is

$$\log p(\mathbf{x}_d|\alpha, \boldsymbol{\beta}) = \log \sum_{\mathbf{z}_d} p(\mathbf{x}_d|\boldsymbol{\beta}, \mathbf{z}_d)p(\mathbf{z}_d|\alpha)$$

$$\geq \mathbb{E}_{q(\mathbf{z}_d|\mathbf{x}_d)}\big[\log p(\mathbf{x}_d|\boldsymbol{\beta}, \mathbf{z}_d)\big] - \mathrm{KL}(q(\mathbf{z}_d|\mathbf{x}_d) \parallel p(\mathbf{z}_d|\alpha)) \equiv \mathcal{L}_d \tag{6}$$

To the best of our knowledge, our proposal is the first VAE for LDA that maximizes the ELBO formulated as in Eq. (6).

The first part of $\mathcal{L}_d$ in Eq. (6) can be rewritten as

$$\mathbb{E}_{q(\mathbf{z}_d|\mathbf{x}_d)}\big[\log p(\mathbf{x}_d|\boldsymbol{\beta}, \mathbf{z}_d)\big] = \sum_{i=1}^{N_d} \mathbb{E}_{q(z_{d,i}|\mathbf{x}_d)}\big[\log \beta_{z_{d,i}, x_{d,i}}\big] \tag{7}$$

where we assume that $q(\mathbf{z}_d|\mathbf{x}_d)$ is factorized as $\prod_{i=1}^{n_d} q(z_{d,i}|\mathbf{x}_d)$ and regard each component $q(z_{d,i}|\mathbf{x}_d)$ as categorical distribution. In this paper, we parameterize $\beta_{k,v}$ as $\beta_{k,v} \propto \exp(\eta_{k,v} + \eta_{0,v})$. The variable $\eta_{0,v}$ is shared by all topics and roughly corresponds to the background probability of the word w_v. The $\eta_{0,v}$'s and the per-topic parameters $\eta_{k,v}$ are estimated directly by maximizing Eq. (7).

The negative KL-divergence in Eq. (6) is given as $-\mathrm{KL}(q(\mathbf{z}_d|\mathbf{x}_d) \parallel p(\mathbf{z}_d|\alpha)) = \mathbb{E}_{q(\mathbf{z}_d|\mathbf{x}_d)}\big[\log p(\mathbf{z}_d|\alpha)\big] - \mathbb{E}_{q(\mathbf{z}_d|\mathbf{x}_d)}\big[\log q(\mathbf{z}_d|\mathbf{x}_d)\big]$. The first half is given as follows by noting that $p(\mathbf{z}_d|\alpha)$ is a Pólya distribution:

$$\mathbb{E}_{q(\mathbf{z}_d|\mathbf{x}_d)}\big[\ln p(\mathbf{z}_d|\alpha)\big] = \mathbb{E}_{q(\mathbf{z}_d|\mathbf{x}_d)}\left[\ln\left\{\frac{(N_d!)\Gamma(K\alpha)}{\Gamma(N_d + K\alpha)} \prod_{k=1}^{K} \frac{\Gamma(n_{d,k} + \alpha)}{(n_{d,k}!)\Gamma(\alpha)}\right\}\right] \tag{8}$$

where $n_{d,k}$ is the number of the word tokens assigned to the topic t_k in $\mathbf{x}_d$. It should be noted that $n_{d,k}$ depends on $\mathbf{z}_d$. The second half of the KL-divergence is an entropy term:

$$-\mathbb{E}_{q(\mathbf{z}_d|\mathbf{x}_d)}\big[\ln q(\mathbf{z}_d|\mathbf{x}_d)\big] = -\sum_{i=1}^{N_d} \mathbb{E}_{q(z_{d,i}|\mathbf{x}_d)}\big[\log q(z_{d,i}|\mathbf{x}_d)\big] \tag{9}$$

The main task in our VAE is to estimate the three expectations in Eqs. (7), (8), and (9) by drawing samples from the approximate posterior $q(\mathbf{z}_d|\mathbf{x}_d)$.

We model the approximate posterior $q(\mathbf{z}_d|\mathbf{x}_d)$ in an amortized manner by using multilayer perceptron (MLP). As already stated, we assume that $q(\mathbf{z}_d|\mathbf{x}_d)$ is factorized as $\prod_{i=1}^{n_d} q(z_{d,i}|\mathbf{x}_d)$ and regard each component $q(z_{d,i}|\mathbf{x}_d)$ as categorical distribution. The parameters of each $q(z_{d,i}|\mathbf{x}_d)$ for $i = 1, \ldots, n_d$ are obtained as follows by using an encoder MLP. Let $\gamma_{d,i} = (\gamma_{d,i,1}, \ldots, \gamma_{d,i,K})$ denote the parameter vector of the categorical distribution $q(z_{d,i}|\mathbf{x}_d)$. That is, $\gamma_{d,i,k}$ is the approximate posterior probability that the i-th word token in the document $\mathbf{x}_d$ is assigned to the topic t_k. We obtain $\gamma_{d,i}$ as the softmaxed output of the encoder MLP. As the input of the encoder for obtaining the approximate posterior parameter vector $\gamma_{d,i}$, we may use the embedding vector of the word $x_{d,i}$.

However, when obtaining $\gamma_{d,i}$ as the softmaxed output of the encoder MLP, the computation should be done by using not only token-wise information but also some document-wide information for a better posterior approximation. If we use no document-wide information, the encoder network cannot make distinction between tokens of the same word appearing in different documents. Therefore, we feed the concatenation of the embedding vector of the i-th word token and the mean of the embedding vectors of all word tokens in $\mathbf{x}_d$ to our MLP. Let $\mathbf{e}_v$ denote the embedding vector of the vocabulary word w_v and $\bar{\mathbf{e}}_d$ denote the mean of the embedding vectors of all word tokens in $\mathbf{x}_d$, i.e., $\bar{\mathbf{e}}_d \equiv \sum_{i=1}^{n_d} \mathbf{e}_{x_{d,i}}/n_d$. Consequently, the approximate posterior parameter $\gamma_{d,i}$ is obtained as $\gamma_{d,i} = \text{Softmax}(\text{MLP}([\mathbf{e}_{x_{d,i}}, \bar{\mathbf{e}}_d]))$, where $[]$ denotes concatenation. It is important to make the estimation of $\gamma_{d,i}$ *context-dependent* in this manner. That is, the estimation of $\gamma_{d,i}$ should be dependent on the word tokens $\{x_{d,1}, \ldots, x_{d,i-1}, x_{d,i+1}, \ldots, x_{d,n_d}\}$ other than $x_{d,i}$ for every i. Further, we make the posterior inference memory efficient by reusing $\eta_{k,v}$, which defines $\beta_{k,v}$, as $e_{v,k}$, i.e., the k-th element of the embedding vector of the word w_v. That is, we tie weights via $e_{v,k} \equiv \eta_{k,v}$. Such weight tying is also used in [16, 17].

We draw samples from $q(z_{d,i}|\mathbf{x}_d)$ with the Gumbel-softmax trick [7]. A discrete sample $z_{d,i} \equiv \text{argmax}_k (g_{d,i,k} + \log \gamma_{d,i,k})$ is approximated by the continuous sample vector $\mathbf{y}_{d,i} = (y_{d,i,1}, \ldots, y_{d,1,K})$ defined by

$$y_{d,i,k} \equiv \frac{\exp((g_{d,i,k} + \log \gamma_{d,i,k})/\tau)}{\sum_{k'} \exp((g_{d,i,k'} + \log \gamma_{d,i,k'})/\tau)} \tag{10}$$

where $g_{d,i,1}, \ldots, g_{d,i,K}$ are the samples from the standard Gumbel distribution Gumbel$(0, 1)$. τ is the temperature parameter to be tuned. We obtain $n_{d,k}$ in Eq. (8) as $n_{d,k} = \sum_{i=1}^{n_d} y_{d,i,k}$. Note that we obtain a different sample for each word token even when more than one tokens of the same word are contained in the same document. That is, the sampling from the approximate posterior is performed in a token-wise manner. However, our encoder MLP accepts not only token-wise embedding information (i.e., $\mathbf{e}_{x_{d,i}}$) but also context-dependent embedding information (i.e., $\bar{\mathbf{e}}_d$). Therefore, we call our method *context-dependent token-wise* variational autoencoder (CTVAE). While we here propose CTVAE only for LDA, a similar proposal can be made for other Bayesian topic models. This would be interesting as future work.

3 Evaluation Experiment

The evaluation used four large document sets, whose specifications are given in Table 1, where D_{train}, D_{valid}, and D_{test} are the sizes of training set, validation

Table 1. Specifications of data sets

	D_{train}	D_{valid}	D_{test}	V
DBLP	2,779,431	346,792	347,291	155,187
PUBMED	5,738,672	1,230,981	1,230,347	141,043
DIET	10,549,675	1,318,663	1,318,805	152,200
NYTimes	239,785	29,978	29,968	102,660

set, and test set, respectively, and V the vocabulary size. DBLP is a subset of the records downloaded from DBLP Web site[3] on July 24, 2018, where each paper title is regarded as document. PUBMED is a part of the bag-of-words data set provided by the UC Irvine Machine Learning Repository.[4] DIET data set is a subset of the Diet Record of both houses of the National Diet of Japan from 1993 to 2012,[5] where each statement by the speaker is regarded as a separate document. Since DIET data set is given in Japanese, we used MeCab morphological analyzer.[6] We also used the NYTimes part from the above-mentioned bag-of-words data set of the UC Irvine Machine Learning Repository.

Our proposal, CTVAE, and all compared methods were implemented in PyTorch.[7] The number of topics was fixed to $K = 50$. All free parameters, including the number of layers and the layer sizes of the encoder MLP, were tuned based on the perplexity computed over the validation set. The perplexity is defined as the exponential of the negative log likelihood of each document, where the log likelihood is normalized by the number of word tokens. The mean of the perplexity over all validation documents was used as the evaluation measure for tuning free parameters. We adopted Adam optimizer [9], where the learning rate scheduling was also tuned based on the validation perplexity.

We compared our proposal to the following three variational inference methods: a plain variational autoencoder (VAE), mini-batch variational Bayes (VB), and adversarial variational Bayes (AVB). Each is explained below.

VAE. While a version of VAE for topic modeling has already been proposed [22], it involves additional elaborations that are not relevant to our comparison. Therefore, we implemented VAE in a more elementary manner by following the topic model in [13]. We adopted the standard multivariate Gaussian distribution as the prior. The variational topic probabilities $\boldsymbol{\theta}_d$ were obtained as $\boldsymbol{\theta}_d \equiv \mathrm{Softmax}(\hat{\boldsymbol{\epsilon}} \odot \boldsymbol{\sigma}(\mathbf{x}_d) + \boldsymbol{\mu}(\mathbf{x}_d))$, where $\hat{\boldsymbol{\epsilon}} \sim \mathcal{N}(\mathbf{0}, \mathbf{1})$. The mini-batch optimization with Adam was conducted for training the encoder MLP, whose output was the concatenation of $\boldsymbol{\mu}(\mathbf{x}_d)$ and $\log \boldsymbol{\sigma}(\mathbf{x}_d)$, and also for updating other parameters. The VAE in our comparison experiment used KL-cost annealing [8,21] and path derivative ELBO gradient [19] along with learning rate scheduling.

---

[3] https://dblp.uni-trier.de/xml/dblp.xml.gz.
[4] https://archive.ics.uci.edu/ml/datasets/bag+of+words.
[5] http://kokkai.ndl.go.jp/.
[6] http://taku910.github.io/mecab/.
[7] https://pytorch.org/.

VB. We also compared our proposal to the variational Bayes (VB) for LDA [1], where no neural network was used. We applied no prior distribution to the per-topic word categorical distributions and directly estimated the per-topic word probabilities by maximizing the data likelihood. We ran a mini-batch version of VB for estimating the per-topic word probabilities. The per-document variational parameters were updated for each document separately in the same manner as [1,6]. While our implementation was based on [6], the optimization was performed in a 'deep learning' manner. That is, we used Adam optimizer, whose learning rate scheduling was tuned based on the validation perplexity.

AVB. We additionally compared CTVAE to adversarial variational Bayes (AVB) [12]. AVB is a variational inference using implicit distribution for approximating the true posterior. The special feature of AVB is that a GAN-like discriminative density ratio estimation [4] is adopted for the estimation of the density ratio between the prior and the variational posterior, which is required for the estimation of the KL-divergence in Eq. (1). Since the AVB described in [12] is not specialized to topic modeling, the AVB proposed for topic modeling [11] was used in our comparison.

Table 2. Evaluation results in terms of test set perplexity

	CTVAE	VAE	AVB	VB
DBLP	1368.63	1749.64	1326.36	**1249.92**
PUBMED	3669.79	1072.63	**991.43**	2958.56
DIET	309.04	364.94	336.33	**219.97**
NYTimes	4077.60	2893.23	**2375.12**	3155.75

Table 2 includes the perplexity computed over the test set for each compared method and each data set. A low perplexity indicates that the approximate posterior is good at predicting word occurrences in test documents. CTVAE improved the test perplexity of VAE both for DBLP and DIET data sets. Especially, CTVAE gave the second best perplexity for DIET data set. Therefore, when VAE does not give any good result, we may use CTVAE as an alternative. AVB gave the best perplexity for PUBMED and NYTimes data sets and was always better than VAE. However, AVB has two MLPs, i.e., the encoder and the discriminator. It is a burden to tune the free parameters for AVB. VB gave the best perplexity for DBLP and DIET data sets. However, VB gave the second worst perplexity for the other two data sets. Further, VB was not efficient in computing test perplexity, because VB required tens of iterations for updating variational parameters until convergence for each document [1] when we computed perplexity over test documents. In contrast, VAE, CTVAE, and AVB only required a single forward computation over the encoder MLP to predict topic probabilities for each unseen document. This was an advantage over VB. As for the wall-clock time of inference, in case of DIET data set, for example, it took 14 h for CTVAE, 10 h for AVB, 7 h for VAE, and 3 h for VB, respectively.

While VAE and AVB only used a single sample for Monte Carlo estimation of the expectations, CTVAE used 10 samples. Therefore, it took more hours to train the encoder MLP in CTVAE. VB was the most efficient in time, because it used no neural networks.

We next present the results of the evaluation of high probability words in each extracted topic in Table 3. We measured the quality of per-topic high probability words with the normalized point-wise mutual information (NPMI) [2], which evaluates how well the co-occurrence of high probability words in each extracted topic reflects the actual word co-occurrence in test documents. NPMI is defined for a pair of words (w, w') as

$$\mathrm{NPMI}(w, w') = \left(\log \frac{p(w, w')}{p(w)p(w')} \right) \Big/ - \log p(w, w') \tag{11}$$

We calculated the probability $p(w)$ as the number of the test documents containing the word w divided by the total number of the test documents and $p(w, w')$ as the number of the test documents containing both w and w' divided by the total number of the test documents. Table 3 includes NPMI computed over the test set by using the top 20 highest probability words from each of the 50 topics. We obtain NPMI for each of the $20(20 - 1)/2 = 190$ word pairs made by pairing two from the top 20 words and then calculate the average over all word pairs from all 50 topics. Larger values are better. As Table 3 shows, the NPMIs for DBLP data set were smaller than the other data sets. This is because the average document length of DBLP data set was much shorter. While CTVAE was worse than VAE in terms of test perplexity for PUBMED and NYTimes data sets, CTVAE was better in terms of NPMI for these two data sets. Especially, CTVAE gave the second best NPMI for NYTimes data set. Table 2 showed that AVB was always better than VAE in terms of perplexity. However, AVB improved the NPMI of VAE only for DBLP and PUBMED data sets. Table 3 shows that VB may be the best choice if we are only interested in the quality of per-topic high probability words and are not interested in the prediction capacity. Table 4 provides an example of high probability words obtained by the compared methods for NYTimes data set. We select seven topics from among the 50 topics and present as many highest probability words for each of the seven topics as the page width allows.

Table 3. Evaluation results in terms of test set NPMI

	CTVAE	VAE	AVB	VB
DBLP	0.0042	0.0358	**0.0622**	0.0177
PUBMED	0.127	0.123	0.190	**0.210**
DIET	0.069	0.096	0.079	**0.116**
NYTimes	0.141	0.105	0.075	**0.218**

Table 4. Highest probability words in randomly chosen seven topics (NYTimes)

CTVAE	play season race win playing fan sport played tour career winning won club winner
	worker officer according cases spokesman security agency operation reported evidence
	ball Lakers NFL NBA dodger season Mets Red_Sox Tiger_Woods ranger Giants
	billion tax bill fund economy economic analyst financial employees investment income
	government Bush federal administration Clinton Congress policy Senate states proposal
	United_States US American foreign China countries Europe Russia european Mexico
	attack war military palestinian terrorist peace gun weapon violence soldier troop
VAE	cup minutes tablespoon add teaspoon oil pepper sugar serving large pan chopped bowl
	Nicholas gift Meryl_Streep Julianne_Moore Oscar Golden_Globes sleigh irish grandfather
	Fed FDA White_House doctor government patient economy rates hospital stock Enron
	yard season game games lead play Giants Dodgers team jet TD touchdown inning goal
	Senator_Mccain Jacques_Chirac Melissa Timothy_Mcveigh Gary_Bauer junk libyan
	expression facial music musical emotion computer brain sound human language memory
	Ed_Belfour Orel_Hershiser John_Smoltz Jerry_Narron Greg_Maddux Tom_Glavine
VB	won win race sport team fight champion winner event match games winning final
	school student teacher college program education class campus children test public
	New_York money Boston director Washington organization New_York_City Manhattan
	America history American century american sense power perhaps word fact public view
	United_States Mexico US Cuba Miami immigrant cuban border country mexican
	Clinton Bush Congress bill White_House administration Senate legislation proposal
	government China political country leader United_States India minister foreign power

(continued)

Table 1. *(continued)*

AVB	Finally spam Margaret_Coker megc eBay Whitney_Houston Michael_Jackson Belarus
	Jack_Welch Keyshawn_Johnson John_McEnroe David_Stern Hideo_Nomo Financial_Times
	Miss_America US_Olympic_Committee Fighters USOC Postal_Service Atlanta_Olympic
	arraigned unsealed striker severance Marsh Equal_Employment_Opportunity_Commission
	rib minutes add cup oil hour tablespoon steak season fish large serving paper fat
	Davos orchid IMF globalization World_Economic_Forum Kyoto capitalism
	learning recognition environments virtual pattern spatial visual matching search text

4   Previous Work

While VAE is widely used in the deep learning field, it is still difficult to apply it to topic modeling, because topic models have discrete latent variables $z_{d,i}$ representing topic assignments. The reparameterization trick [10, 18, 20, 24] cannot be straightforwardly applied to discrete variables. Therefore, low-variance gradient estimation for discrete variables is realized by using some elaborated technique [25] or the Gumbel-softmax trick [7]. The existing proposals of variational inference for topic modeling in the deep learning field [3, 13, 22, 26] marginalize out the discrete variables $z_{d,i}$ and only consider continuous variables. In contrast, CTVAE marginalizes out the topic probabilities $\theta_{d,k}$. This marginalizing out is also performed in the Gibbs sampling [5], the collapsed variational Bayes [23], and the variational inference proposed by [15]. This paper follows [15] and proposes a new VAE for topic modeling. It is also an important contribution of this paper to prove empirically that the Gumbel-softmax trick works also for the discrete latent variables $z_{d,i}$ in topic modeling.

5   Conclusions

We propose a new variational autoencoder for topic modeling, called context-dependent token-wise variational autoencoder (CTVAE), by marginalizing out the per-document topic probabilities. The main feature of CTVAE is that the sampling from the variational posterior is performed in a token-wise manner with respect to the context specified by each document. The context is represented as the mean of the embedding vectors of the word tokens in each document. This feature led to the test perplexity better than the existing VAE proposals for some data sets. However, the improvement was not remarkable. It is an important future research direction to improve the performance of CTVAE. One reason why the improvement was mediocre is that the context information given to the encoder was not effective. By marginalizing out the topic probabilities $\theta_{d,k}$, we make the token-wise topic assignments $z_{d,i}$ in the same document mutually dependent. Therefore, we should make the encoder output reflect the dependency of the topic assignment $z_{d,i}$ on all other topic assignments $\mathbf{z}_d \setminus z_{d,i}$. This paper indeed shows that even under a simple factorization assumption, i.e., under the assumption that $q(\mathbf{z}_d|\mathbf{x}_d) = \prod_i q(z_{d,i}|\mathbf{x}_d)$, we could obtain an interesting result only by using the mean word embedding vector $\bar{\mathbf{e}}_d$ as a part of the encoder input. However, we need a better way to make the encoder output reflect the dependency among the $z_{d,i}$'s.

Acknowledgment. This work was supported by JSPS KAKENHI Grant Number JP18K11440.

References

1. Blei, D.M., Ng, A.Y., Jordan, M.I.: Latent Dirichlet allocation. J. Mach. Learn. Res. **3**, 993–1022 (2003)
2. Bouma, G.: Normalized (Pointwise) Mutual information in collocation extraction. In: Proceedings of the Biennial GSCL Conference From Form to Meaning: Processing Texts Automatically, vol. 2009, pp. 31–40 (2009)
3. Dieng, A.B., Wang, C., Gao, J., Paisley, J.W.: TopicRNN: a recurrent neural network with long-range semantic dependency. CoRR abs/1611.01702 (2016). http://arxiv.org/abs/1611.01702
4. Goodfellow, I.J., et al.: Generative adversarial nets. In: Advances in Neural Information Processing Systems, vol. 27 (NIPS), pp. 2672–2680 (2014)
5. Griffiths, T.L., Steyvers, M.: Finding scientific topics. Proc. Nat. Acad. Sci. **101**(suppl 1), 5228–5235 (2004)
6. Hoffman, M.D., Blei, D.M., Bach, F.R.: Online learning for latent Dirichlet allocation. Adv. Neural Inf. Process. Syst. (NIPS) **23**, 856–864 (2010)
7. Jang, E., Gu, S., Poole, B.: Categorical reparameterization with Gumbel-softmax. CoRR abs/1611.01144 (2016), http://arxiv.org/abs/1611.01144
8. Kim, Y., Wiseman, S., Miller, A.C., Sontag, D., Rush, A.M.: Semi-amortized variational autoencoders. In: Proceedings of the 35th International Conference on Machine Learning (ICML), pp. 2683–2692 (2018)
9. Kingma, D.P., Ba, J.: Adam: A method for stochastic optimization. CoRR abs/1412.6980 (2014). http://arxiv.org/abs/1412.6980
10. Kingma, D.P., Welling, M.: Auto-encoding variational Bayes. CoRR abs/1312.6114 (2013). http://arxiv.org/abs/1312.6114
11. Masada, T., Takasu, A.: Adversarial learning for topic models. In: Proceedings of the 14th International Conference on Advanced Data Mining and Applications (ADMA), pp. 292–302 (2018)
12. Mescheder, L.M., Nowozin, S., Geiger, A.: Adversarial variational Bayes: unifying variational autoencoders and generative adversarial networks. In: Proceedings of the 34th International Conference on Machine Learning (ICML), pp. 2391–2400 (2017)

13. Miao, Y., Grefenstette, E., Blunsom, P.: Discovering discrete latent topics with neural variational inference. In: Proceedings of the 34th International Conference on Machine Learning (ICML), pp. 2410–2419 (2017)
14. Miao, Y., Yu, L., Blunsom, P.: Neural variational inference for text processing. In: Proceedings of the 33rd International Conference on Machine Learning (ICML), pp. 1727–1736 (2016)
15. Mimno, D., Hoffman, M.D., Blei, D.M.: Sparse stochastic inference for latent Dirichlet allocation. In: Proceedings of the 29th International Conference on Machine Learning (ICML), pp. 1515–1522 (2012)
16. Mnih, A., Hinton, G.E.: A scalable hierarchical distributed language model. Adv. Neural Inf. Process. Syst. (NIPS) **21**, 1081–1088 (2008)
17. Press, O., Wolf, L.: Using the output embedding to improve language models. CoRR abs/1608.05859 (2016). http://arxiv.org/abs/1608.05859
18. Rezende, D.J., Mohamed, S., Wierstra, D.: Stochastic backpropagation and approximate inference in deep generative models. In: Proceedings of the 31st International Conference on Machine Learning (ICML), pp. II-1278-II-1286 (2014)
19. Roeder, G., Wu, Y., Duvenaud, D.K.: Sticking the landing: simple, lower-variance gradient estimators for variational inference. Adv. Neural Inf. Process. Syst. (NIPS) **30**, 6928–6937 (2017)
20. Salimans, T., Knowles, D.A.: Fixed-form variational posterior approximation through stochastic linear regression. CoRR abs/1206.6679 (2012). http://arxiv.org/abs/1206.6679
21. Sønderby, C.K., Raiko, T., Maaløe, L., Sønderby, S.K., Winther, O.: Ladder variational autoencoders. Adv. Neural Inf. Process. Syst. (NIPS) **29**, 3738–3746 (2016)
22. Srivastava, A., Sutton, C.: Autoencoding variational inference for topic models. CoRR abs/1703.01488 (2017). http://arxiv.org/abs/1703.01488
23. Teh, Y.W., Newman, D., Welling, M.: A collapsed variational Bayesian inference algorithm for latent Dirichlet allocation. Adv. Neural Inf. Process. Syst. (NIPS) **19**, 1353–1360 (2006)
24. Titsias, M.K., Lázaro-Gredilla, M.: Doubly stochastic variational Bayes for non-conjugate inference. In: Proceedings of the 31st International Conference on Machine Learning (ICML), pp. II-1971-II-1980 (2014)
25. Tokui, S., Sato, I.: Reparameterization trick for discrete variables. CoRR abs/1611.01239 (2016). http://arxiv.org/abs/1611.01239
26. Wang, W., et al.: Topic compositional neural language model. In: Proceedings of the 21st International Conference on Artificial Intelligence and Statistics (AISTATS), pp. 356–365 (2018)

Extraction of Relations Between Entities from Human-Generated Content on Social Networks

Marco Adriani, Marco Brambilla, and Marco Di Giovanni[✉]

Politecnico di Milano, via Ponzio 34/5, 20133 Milano, Italy
marco1.adriani@mail.polimi.it,
{marco.brambilla,marco.digiovanni}@polimi.it

Abstract. In this work, we present a method to extract new knowledge from content shared by users on social networks, with particular emphasis on extraction of evolving relations between entities. Our method combines natural language processing and machine learning for extracting relations in the form of triples (subject-relation-object). The method works on domain-specific content shared on social networks: users can define a domain through a set of criteria (social networks accounts, keywords or hashtags) and they can define a limited set of relations that are of interest for the given domain. Based on this input, our method extracts the relevant triples for the domain. The method is demonstrated on content retrieved from Twitter, belonging to different domain-specific scenarios, like fashion and chess. Results are promising, in terms of both precision and recall.

Keywords: Knowledge extraction · Natural language processing · Social network analysis · Knowlwedge base

1 Introduction

In recent years, large knowledge bases (KBs) have been built, organizing large amounts of information in such a way to make it easily accessible to both humans and machines. Notable examples are DBpedia [2], the Google Knowledge Graph, and Yago [19]. As [3] pointed out, a problem with such tools is that knowledge evolves very fast and they are not designed to automatically deal with this. Indeed, the process of ontological knowledge discovery [15] tends to focus on the most popular or established items, those which are mostly quoted or referenced (which we call *high-frequency* items), and it is less effective in discovering less popular items, those belonging to the long tail (i.e., the *low frequency* items, that appear less frequently in the discussions). Therefore, some information is not captured in knowledge bases because, for instance, it is not sufficiently popular on the Web. A possible way to address this problem is to look at other data sources, like social media sites, containing *social content*, continuously created by people, and that can thus describe new facts as soon as they happen [16,18].

© Springer Nature Switzerland AG 2020
M. Brambilla et al. (Eds.): ICWE 2019 Workshops, LNCS 11609, pp. 48–60, 2020.
https://doi.org/10.1007/978-3-030-51253-8_7

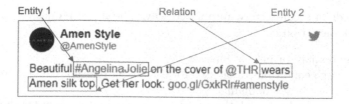

Fig. 1. Example of tweet and relation extracted between two objects.

We present a method to extract new knowledge from social content, with particular emphasis on **extraction of binary relationships emerging from textual statements shared on social networks**.

Various researches targeted the general version of this problem already [8, 9,14]. However, many of them only extracted generic relations, without caring about the naming or typing of the relations. Others obtained limited accuracy, also due to the generality of the problem addressed: for instance [7] applied syntax-based techniques to the general problem of relation extraction.

In this work we take a particular angle to the problem, that is: we focus on specific domains of interest, and then we aim at a refined extraction, that also focuses on understanding the type of relation that is detected, out of a given set of domain-relevant relations, in a way similar to the approach discussed in [5] for emerging entity extraction.

Given a short text shared by humans on social networks, we aim at identifying the main relation defined in the statement, together with the two entities it connects. Our approach aims at being resilient to the typical style of social network communication, which includes informal style, partial incorrect syntax, truncated sentences and so on. The simplicity and compactness of social network communication leads to having most of the contributions actually including only one important relation. Our approach is based on machine learning combined with natural language processing techniques. Knowledge will be modeled as a list of triples, so as to easily reuse the generated knowledge to enrich existing triple knowledge bases (for instance, implemented as RDF repositories).

Notice that we go beyond understanding the presence of a verbal phrase encoding a relation: we want to determine the belonging of the relation to a general category of verbal associations that describe the "same kind" of association between entities. As an example, Fig. 1 shows the text of a tweet shared by a user ("*@AmenStyle*") on Twitter, and highlights the relation (*to wear*) and the two entities it connects ("*Angelina Jolie*" and "*Amen silk top*"). In this example, we determine the relation as "wearing". However, we want to represent as "wearing" also any other kind of expression that represent the same idea. For instance, a man dressed up for a party with a tuxedo, is also "wearing" the tuxedo, and thus the relation must be the same.

We present a simple rule-based approach as a baseline and improve over that with a method based on Machine Learning techniques. Our method keeps the human in the loop for the definition of the initial setting of the extraction, and then proceeds in a completely automated way. The input requested to the user includes the definition of:

1. a specific domain or field of interest;
2. a set of search conditions to be used for retrieving relevant content from social media for the chosen domain;
3. a limited set of relevant relations that are deemed interesting for the domain.

Based on this, our techniques extracts the triples representing instances of the relations of interest together with the connected objects.

The paper is organized as follows: Sect. 2 presents our hybrid approach proposed to extract relations from social content. Section 3 reports on our experiments on two domains of interest. Section 4 discusses the related work and Sect. 5 concludes.

2   Methodology for Extraction of Relations

Our approach to relation extraction from social media is based on a few main phases. After a preliminary data cleaning and preprocessing phase, each social media post is processed for extracting the syntactic structure of the sentence (as far as possible, considering that the social media posts are often featuring broken or partial phrases), and then applies the actual extraction steps, which determine the main relation and the entities connected through it. Finally, the triple describing the whole relation is composed.

1. **Preprocessing.** Since text retrieved from social networks can be noisy due to the presence of unwanted words, URLs, tags, etc., so that it can mislead syntactic analysis tools, we apply text cleaning over the content. Among others, we remove URLs, replace HTML Entities with the corresponding characters, and remove the "@" and "#" tokens.
2. **Syntactic Analysis.** We proceed analyzing the syntactic structure of the posts, by applying part-of-speech tagging and syntax tree generation[1].
3. **Relation Extraction.** The content is analyzed to find the main relation expressed within the text.
4. **Subject and Object Extraction.** The content is analyzed to find the subject and object of the relation found by the previous phase.
5. **Composition of Triple.** After extracting subject, object and relation, we combine them to form the triples. Since multiple (or no) elements may be found for any of the placehoders, some non-trivial decisions are made in this phase too. For instance, some heuristics are introduced for determining the subject in case it's not explicitly defined in the text.

---

[1] We use the POS-tagging implementation provided by SyntaxNet, a TensorFlow toolkit for natural language processing available at https://github.com/tensorflow/models/tree/master/research/syntaxnet.

Table 1. Rules implemented for the extraction in the baseline rule-based approach.

Position		ROOT	CHILD 1	CHILD 2
Rule 1	*Role*	**Relation**	**Subject**	**Object**
	Dependency rel.	Root	Nominal subject	Clausal complement
				Direct, passive or ind. obj
	POS tag	Verb	Noun or pronoun	Noun, pronoun or adj.
Rule 2	*Role*	**Object**	**Subject**	**Relation**
	Dependency rel.	Clausal compl	Nominal subject	Copula
	POS tag	Adjective	Noun or pronoun	Verb
Rule 3	*Role*	**Relation**	**Subject**	**Object**
	Dependency rel.	Clausal compl	Nominal subject	Direct, passive or ind. obj
	POS tag	Verb	Noun or pronoun	Noun or pronoun
Rule 4	*Role*	**Object**	**Subject**	**Relation**
	Dependency rel.	Adv. clause modifier	Nominal subject	Copula
	POS tag	Adjective	Noun	Verb
			Pronoun	

Notice that we go beyond understanding the presence of a verbal phrase encoding a relation: we want to determine the belonging of the relation to a general category of verbal associations that describe the "same kind" of relation between entities, that is particularly relevant for the given domain.

For our analysis, we implement and compare two techniques: a rule-based approach, which is used as a baseline in our experiments, and our hybrid syntactic and learning approach. We describe how the main steps of the process (extraction and composition of triples) are defined in both cases.

2.1   Rule-Based Approach (Baseline)

The baseline approach consists of a simple method to directly extract all triples from a list of posts, starting from the POS tagging of the sentence. We use the dependency tree generated by the POS tagger as input. The rules exploit the tag of the words and their relative position in the dependency tree as variables, and they determine how they map to the three roles in the triple to be generated. Each of them finds a full triple. The rules directly extract the three components of the triple, by extracting a sub-tree from the syntactic tree of the post, composed by a root and two children, each representing a subject, an object or a relation. In a sense, the rules represent "templates" of possible triples. If any of the components is not identified, the triple is not detected. As a baseline we define a set of 4 rules as reported in Table 1.

The rules used by this approach were empirically derived from the analysis of the typical syntactic structures of the posts in the dataset. This approach could be extended by including more rules and/or more general or powerful rules, for instance considering also multi-level sub-trees. However, by adding more rules, the number of wrongly extracted triples could get higher, because some rules would be triggered even in the wrong cases. This set of rules has been identified empirically to be a good trade-off.

This approach merge together the relation extraction step and the subject and object extraction step.

2.2 Machine Learning Approach

A machine learning approach is also proposed, where, instead of creating empirically a set of rules as in the Baseline approach (Sect. 2.1), a supervised algorithm is trained to extract relations, subjects and objects.

As already noted, the ML approach consists of two main steps: *Relation extraction* and *Subject and object extraction*.

Relation Extraction. The task of the relation extraction step is to find the main relation of a post, given the text, its syntactic structure and the list of selected relations. We assume that each post contains a single relation. Firstly, one of the selected relations is assigned to each post, using a multi-class classification. Then, the text is analyzed to find which verb corresponds to the assigned relation. This verb will correspond the main relation of the post.

The text of each post is initially converted to a numerical feature vector, splitting it in tokens, removing stopwords, converting each word to its base form (e.g., "is" gets converted to "be") and applying a variant of Bag of Words. Once converted, it can be used as input for a multi-class classifier.

We employed a set of linear SVM classifiers, using the *One-against-One* approach to make them work with a multi-class problem. To train the classifier, human generated labels were used.

Once a relation is assigned to each post, if the relation is not categorized as "OTHER", the corresponding verb is searched in the text. If no verb corresponding to the assigned relation is found, the post is skipped.

Subject and Object Extraction. The task of the subject and object extraction step is to find a list of subjects and objects for each post that, later, will be composed in triples, adding the relation already found in the previous step.

Finding subjects and objects is done by first converting the words of each post to a feature vector, expressing the meaning of the word and its relations with the other words of the same post. Such feature vector, whose structure is shown in Fig. 2, contains a coarse-grained Part Of Speech (POS) tag (e.g., noun, adjective, verb), a fine-grained one (e.g., singular/plural noun, base/comparative form adjective, base form/past tense verb), the relation between the word and its root in the syntax tree (e.g., nominal subject, direct object), whether the word is the main relation of the post, the signed difference in tree level from the main relation of the post and the distance, in terms of number of words, between the word and the main relation of the post. These features provide information about both the meaning of the word (semantic) and the structural proprieties of the text (encoded in the tree representation).

Once the words are converted in feature vectors, a multi-class classifier is used to decide, for every word, whether it is a subject, an object or something else.

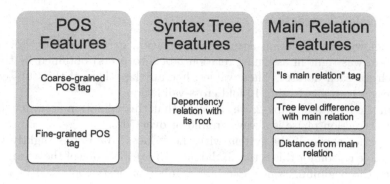

Fig. 2. Organization of the feature vector used for the analysis of each word.

Table 2. Validation accuracy for Relation extraction, using ML approach.

Fashion	Chess
82.4%	*68.5%*

For this step, we tried two classification models: a set of nonlinear SVMs with Gaussian kernel, combined with the *One-against-One* approach, and a Random Forest (RF) algorithm with 10 decision trees, whose output is computed using majority vote among the trees. The output are lists of words classified as subjects or objects.

3 Experiments

To validate the quality of our work, we ran some experiments, applying the described approaches to two different English datasets taken from Twitter, belonging to two different domains (fashion and chess). For the fashion domain (containing around 4000 posts by designers, stylists and photographers), we extracted a random sample of 650 tweets. For the chess domain (containing around 9000 posts by some of the top chess players), we extracted a sample of 700 tweets. In both cases, we assessed through manual evaluation that around 65% of the posts contained verbs associated to the relations we were looking for, while the remaining posts contained only *generic* verbs.

For the ML approaches, in addition to the *final* results, that consider the number of correct triples returned by the *Triples composition* step, we report metrics describing the quality of the *intermediate* results (i.e., those of the *Relation extraction* and *Subject and object extraction* steps). In this way, it is possible to understand both how well the whole approach works, and which kind of behavior is exhibited by its main components.

To make reading easier, in the following tables, the best results are highlighted in **bold**, and the second-best results in *italic*.

3.1 Relation Extraction

Table 2 shows the validation accuracy for relation extraction (i.e., how often the system was right in assigning relation labels to posts) obtained by the ML approach for each dataset. These values, like all the others of this sub-section, are averages computed using 10-fold cross-validation.

From the results in Table 2, we can note that the validation accuracy for the relation extraction phase is always around or over 70%.

The performance of the system with the "Chess" dataset is slightly worse. One possible reason for this is that it did not fully respect one of the assumptions stated at the beginning, since a certain number of posts contained more than one "main relation".

In Table 3 and 4, the *per-relation* results obtained by the ML approach for each relation are shown. The metrics reported in the tables are:

- *Per-relation precision*, defined as the number of posts *correctly* labeled with a given relation divided by the total number of posts labeled with that relation;
- *Per-relation recall*, defined as the number of posts *correctly* labeled with a given relation divided by the number of posts containing that relation that are present in the dataset.

Table 3. Per-relation precision and recall for fashion domain, using ML approach.

Relation	Fashion	
	Precision	Recall
WEAR	**90.1%**	**94.1%**
PH	59.4%	45.2%
LIKE	74.0%	78.6%
CREATE	76.9%	58.8%
OTHER	*84.2%*	*85.7%*

Table 4. Per-relation precision and recall for chess domain, using ML approach.

Relation	Chess	
	Precision	Recall
PLAY	41.5%	42.2%
LOSE	50.7%	65.5%
LIKE	*70.5%*	*69.7%*
WIN	64.4%	52.1%
OTHER	**75.9%**	**75.4%**

Based on the results shown in the previous tables, we can make some considerations. The performance of the non-"OTHER" relations is quite variable, and this can almost always be traced to differences in the number of posts containing each relation: indeed, the more examples of a relation we have, the better the algorithm will be accurate in predicting it.

The "OTHER" relation shows the best overall performance among all the datasets. This is expected, because it is the most diffused one, by a wide margin.

From the confusion matrices corresponding to these results, we further noticed that the relations different from "OTHER" are mostly confused with "OTHER" , and not between each other. This means that, once the system manages to correctly recognize a post as not belonging to "OTHER" (as it is most of the times), then it usually assigns it to the right relation.

For the chess dataset (Table 4), the relation with the worst performance is "PLAY" , that is also quite "generic" from a semantic point of view and partially overlaps with "WIN" and "LOSE". This sound reasonable because, if a class does not have a well-defined "shape", it will be harder for the classifier to learn how to recognize it and reinforces the idea that a proper choice of the selected relations is important to get good performance.

Table 5. Validation accuracy for subject and object extraction, using SVM and RF.

Dataset	SVM	RF
Fashion	**93.7%**	*93.0%*
Chess	*95.1%*	**95.4%**

Table 6. Per-output precision and recall using SVM.

Output	Fashion		Chess	
	Precision	Recall	Precision	Recall
SUBJECT	*85.0%*	*73.9%*	*80.2%*	*70.8%*
OBJECT	79.5%	71.0%	78.1%	62.4%
OTHER	**95.4%**	**97.3%**	**96.5%**	**98.2%**

3.2 Subject and Object Extraction

Table 5 shows the validation accuracy for subject and object extraction (i.e., how often the system was right in deciding whether a given word was a subject, an object, or something else) obtained by the ML approach for each dataset, using both the SVM and RF classification models.

These values, like all the others of this sub-section, are averages computed using 10-fold cross-validation.

We can note that the validation accuracy for subject and object extraction is between 93% and 95% , regardless of the considered dataset and classification model. This is a quite good result; however, in this case, it is very important to look at the *per-output* precision and recall, to have a good indication of the real performance of the system.

Indeed, since the system is trying to correctly extract a small (between 10% and 15%) subset of the input samples (i.e., the words that are either subjects or objects in their post), an easy way for the classifiers to obtain a high validation accuracy would be by assigning all the samples to the "OTHER" output: not a desirable outcome.

In Table 6 and Table 7, the *per-output* results for this phase are thus shown, for each dataset and classification model. The metrics reported in the tables are:

Table 7. Per-output precision and recall using ML approach with RF.

Output	Fashion		Chess	
	Precision	Recall	Precision	Recall
SUBJECT	*79.3%*	*73.9%*	*82.0%*	*75.8%*
OBJECT	77.4%	68.8%	80.3%	60.8%
OTHER	**95.2%**	**96.7%**	**96.6%**	**98.4%**

Table 8. Precision and recall for the various datasets and approaches.

Approach	Fashion		Chess	
	Precision	Recall	Precision	Recall
Baseline	61.5%	29.3%	50.5%	32.0%
SVM	*66.9%*	*58.1%*	**68.9%**	*58.3%*
RF	**73.7%**	**67.5%**	*66.7%*	**62.9%**

– *Per-output precision*, defined as the number of words *correctly* labeled as subject/object/other divided by the total number of words labeled as, respectively, subject, object or "other" ;
– *Per-output recall*, defined as the number of words *correctly* labeled as subject/object/other divided by the number of words, present in the dataset, that *actually* are, respectively, a subject, an object or something else.

Looking at the tables, we can make some considerations.

As it is usually the case with these methods, the best results are obtained on the most diffused output, "OTHER". However, the results for "SUBJECT" and "OBJECT", while being far from what the overall validation accuracy was suggesting, are not bad: the precision is almost always over 75% with a recall around 70%.

We can note that it seems easier, for both classification models and on all samplings, to correctly recognize subjects than objects, in terms of both precision and recall.

About the two considered approaches, we see that the SVM shows slightly better overall performance than RF on the fashion datasets, while the opposite is true for the chess one. They showed equivalent performance on the "OTHER" output.

Overall, the two approaches offer similar performance.

3.3   Final Results

In Table 8, we report the results achieved by the three discussed approaches (Baseline, VM and RF) on the two datasets (*Fashion* and *Chess*) considering the following metrics:

- *Precision*, defined as the number of correctly extracted triples divided by the total number of extracted triples;
- *Recall*, defined as the number of correctly extracted triples divided by the number of triples present in the dataset.

These values are averages computed using 3-fold cross-validation.

From the results, we can note that the baseline method achieves precision between 50% and 62% , depending on the dataset, with recall around 30%.

The ML approach significantly improves over the baseline, in terms of both precision and recall, for every dataset: for instance, with Random Forest, the improvement on precision is between 12% and 17% , depending on the dataset, while for recall it is between 31% and 39%.

The *shape* of the result is somehow expected because the baseline is implemented using *fixed rules*, that, while being able to achieve a certain degree of precision, cannot easily cover the many ways triples can be present in a piece of text, without becoming too numerous, complex and difficult to build by hand.

What we see from the results is that, instead, Machine Learning methods can *automatically* understand the rules that have to be used to extract triples out of social content.

In general, we see that using Random Forest to extract subjects and objects provides slightly better results with respect to Support Vector Machines, but, in many cases, the performance of the two classifiers is quite close.

We can finally note that results of the chess domain are slightly worse with respect to the fashion one. As already noted, one possible reason for this is that it did not fully respect one of the assumptions stated at the beginning, since a certain number of posts were found to contain more than one "main relation".

4 Related Work

Many approaches and tools exist for performing knowledge extraction and ontology learning [11]. The relevance of *Social Media Analytics* (SMA) as interdisciplinary research field is described extensively in [18], which also analyzes the current challenges of SMA research and points out the importance of an interdisciplinary research agenda. In [16], an ontology enrichment pipeline is proposed, that can automatically augment an existing domain-specific ontology using data extracted by a crawler from social media applications. In [20], the so-called *Social Awareness Streams* approach shows that some kinds of social streams may be more suitable for some knowledge retrieval tasks than others.

Seminal works on the knowledge extraction problem applied fuzzy rules [13]. Other approaches apply ontology based techniques [1], more recently integrated with others, such as discourse representation theory [17]. Indeed, mixed approaches showed a positive impact on the quality of the results. For instance, [10] applies a two-stage process to semantic extraction, with a first shallow extraction that is subsequently refined with statistical and semantic analysis.

A few works address the problem of relation extraction. The paper [9] applies supervised knowledge extraction, aimed at detecting entities, relations between them and events from text, audio and image data. The paper [14] proposeS extraction of information regarding trending events, starting from content posted on Twitter, represented with a *subject-predicate-object* model. The approach combines existing NLP-based named entity recognition and relation extraction tools. [8] extracts semantics of tweets in the shape *entity-relation-entity* by linking Twitter posts to related news articles and using both sources to find limited relations between entities. Some works apply syntactical and structural analysis of the sentence for extracting relations [6], while others subsequently explore integration with lexical graphs like WordNet [12]. Other works focus on very specific cases of relations (e.g., [21] covers only relations between people and companies). Many of these approaches apply kernel function based approaches to the problem.

The work described in this paper is defined in the context of a broader vision on knowledge discovery, presented in [3]. Other works defined in the same context described the extraction of emerging entities [5], and iterative approaches to extraction of evolving knowledge [4]. The work [7] already addressed the specific problem we address here (relation extraction), but it proposed a general-purpose rule-based solution over the structure of the syntactic tree of the sentences, which lead to limited quality of results.

5   Conclusions

We proposed an approach that is able to retrieve triples representing semantic binary relations between concepts from social media content using NLP and Machine Learning. We showed that the method is feasible and provides good performance when put at work on real world domains.

Future works will concentrate on relaxing the required assumptions (e.g., the assumption of one single "main relation" for each post) and performing further validations with data coming from different sources (e.g., Facebook, Instagram). Moreover, we would also like to explore the possibility to integrate our system in a pipeline for knowledge base enrichment, for instance determining if the entities involved in the relation (and the relation itself) are already recorded in the KB.

Acknowledgements. This work was partially funded by: Regione Lombardia POR-FESR Project "FaST (Fashion Sensing Technology) - ID 187010". We thank the Fashion In Process group (http://www.fashioninprocess.com/the-collective) of Politecnico di Milano for the discussions on the fashion domain use case.

References

1. Alani, H., et al.: Automatic ontology-based knowledge extraction from web documents. IEEE Intell. Syst. **18**(1), 14–21 (2003)
2. Bizer, C., et al.: Dbpedia - a crystallization point for the web of data. Web Semantics: Sci. Serv. Agents World Wide Web **7**(3), 154–165 (2009)

3. Brambilla, M., Ceri, S., Daniel, F., Della Valle, E.: On the quest for changing knowledge. In: Proceedings of the Workshop on Data-Driven Innovation on the Web DDI@WebSci, colocated with Web Science 2016, Hannover, Germany, 22–25 May 2016, pp. 3:1–3:5 (2016)
4. Brambilla, M., Ceri, S., Daniel, F., Di Giovanni, M., Mauri, A., Ramponi, G.: Iterative knowledge extraction from social networks. In: The Web Conference, WWW2018, Lyon. pp. 1359–1364 (2018)
5. Brambilla, M., Ceri, S., Della Valle, E., Volonterio, R., Acero Salazar, F.X.: Extracting emerging knowledge from social media. In: Proceedings of the 26th International Conference on World Wide Web, WWW 2017, Perth, Australia, pp. 795–804 (2017)
6. Bunescu, R.C., Mooney, R.J.: A shortest path dependency kernel for relation extraction. In: Proceedings of Conference on Human Language Technology and Empirical Methods in NLP, pp. 724–731. HLT 2005, Association for Comp. Linguistics (2005)
7. Caielli, A., Brambilla, M., Ceri, S., Daniel, F.: Harvesting knowledge from social networks: extracting typed relationships among entities. In: Garrigós, I., Wimmer, M. (eds.) ICWE 2017. LNCS, vol. 10544, pp. 223–227. Springer, Cham (2018). https://doi.org/10.1007/978-3-319-74433-9_20
8. Celik, I., Abel, F., Houben, G.-J.: Learning semantic relationships between entities in Twitter. In: Auer, S., Díaz, O., Papadopoulos, G.A. (eds.) ICWE 2011. LNCS, vol. 6757, pp. 167–181. Springer, Heidelberg (2011). https://doi.org/10.1007/978-3-642-22233-7_12
9. Doddington, G., Mitchell, A., Przybocki, M., Ramshaw, L., Strassel, S., Weischedel, R.: The automatic content extraction (ACE) program - tasks, data, and evaluation. In: Proceedings of the Fourth International Conference on Language Resources and Evaluation (LREC'04). European Language Resources Association (ELRA), Lisbon, Portugal, May 2004). http://www.lrec-conf.org/proceedings/lrec2004/pdf/5.pdf
10. Fan, J., Kalyanpur, A., Gondek, D.C., Ferrucci, D.A.: Automatic knowledge extraction from documents. IBM J. Res. Dev. 56(3.4), 5:1–5:10 (2012)
11. Gangemi, A.: A comparison of knowledge extraction tools for the semantic web. In: The Semantic Web: Semantics and Big Data. pp. 351–366. Springer, Berlin (2013)
12. GuoDong, Z., Jian, S., Jie, Z., Min, Z.: Exploring various knowledge in relation extraction. In: Proceedings of the 43rd Annual Meeting on Association for Computational Linguistics. pp. 427–434. ACL 2005, Association for Computational Linguistics, Stroudsburg (2005)
13. Jin, Y., von Seelen, W., Sendhoff, B.: An approach to rule-based knowledge extraction. In: 1998 IEEE International Conference on Fuzzy Systems Proceedings. IEEE World Congress on Computational Intelligence (Cat. No.98CH36228). vol. 2, pp. 1188–1193, vol. 2, May 1998
14. Katsios, G., Vakulenko, S., Krithara, A., Paliouras, G.: Towards open domain event extraction from twitter: revealing entity relations. In: 4th Internatioanl Workshop on Detection, Representation, and Exploitation of Events in the Semantic Web (DeRiVE) at ESWC 2015, p. 35–46 (2015)
15. Maedche, A.: Ontology Learning for the Semantic Web, vol. 665. Springer, Boston (2012). https://doi.org/10.1007/978-1-4615-0925-7
16. Monachesi, P., Markus, T.: Using social media for ontology enrichment. In: Aroyo, L., et al. (eds.) ESWC 2010. LNCS, vol. 6089, pp. 166–180. Springer, Heidelberg (2010). https://doi.org/10.1007/978-3-642-13489-0_12

17. Presutti, V., Draicchio, F., Gangemi, A.: Knowledge extraction based on discourse representation theory and linguistic frames. In: Teiji, A., et al. (eds.) EKAW 2012. LNCS (LNAI), vol. 7603, pp. 114–129. Springer, Heidelberg (2012). https://doi.org/10.1007/978-3-642-33876-2_12
18. Stieglitz, S., Dang-Xuan, L., Bruns, A., Neuberger, C.: Social media analytics - an interdisciplinary approach and its implications for information systems. Bus. Inf. Syst. Eng. 6, 89–96 (2014)
19. Suchanek, F.M., Kasneci, G., Weikum, G.: Yago: A core of semantic knowledge. In: Proceedings of the 16th International Conference on World Wide Web, pp. 697–706. WWW 2007, ACM, New York (2007)
20. Wagner, C., Strohmaier, M.: The wisdom in tweetonomies: acquiring latent conceptual structures from social awareness streams. In: SEMSEARCH 2010. ACM (2010)
21. Zelenko, D., Aone, C., Richardella, A.: Kernel methods for relation extraction. J. Mach. Learn. Res. 3, 1083–1106 (2003)

Social Networks as Communication Channels: A Logical Approach

Matteo Cristani[1]($\boxtimes$), Francesco Olivieri[2], and Katia Santacà[1]

[1] Department of Computer Science, University of Verona, Verona, Italy
matteo.cristani@univr.it
[2] Data61, CSIRO, Brisbane, Australia

Abstract. Agents use channels to communicate publicly. An agent announcing a statement on a communication channel poses non trivial questions about the nature of such a statement as well as about the attitude of the agent herself. Does the agent know whether the statement is true? Is this agent announcing that statement or its contrary in any other channel?

Extensions to Dynamic Epistemic Logics have been proposed in the recent past that give account to public announcements. One major limit of these logics is that announcements are always considered truthful. It is however clear that, in real life, incompetent agents may announce false things, while deceitful agents may even announce things they do not believe in.

In this paper, we shall provide a logical framework, called Multiple Channel Logic, able to relate true statements, agent beliefs, and announcements on communication channels. We discuss syntax and semantics of this logic and show the behaviour of the proposed deduction system. Lastly, we shall present a classification of agents based on the above introduced behaviour analysis.

1 Introduction

The late evolution of the Internet has exploited a number of novel reasoning problems. In several approaches to reasoning about web processes, two different matters tend to intersect: the attitudes of the agents using the web for communication activities, and the beliefs of those agents. Consider, in particular, a situation in which a set of agents use many different communication channels, as for instance blogs, social networks, forums. It may happen that these agents use those channels in an incoherent way: for instance one agent may announce one statement in a channel while omitting it in another one, or she can announce a statement in a channel and the opposite statement in another one.

There are two different forms of incoherence. We can look at different agents announcing opposite statements (a situation that we name *relational incoherence*), or only onto incoherences of one single agent (that we name *internal incoherence*). Both types of incoherence lie on the same ground: contradictory statements are made. The former type involves different agents making such

© Springer Nature Switzerland AG 2020
M. Brambilla et al. (Eds.): ICWE 2019 Workshops, LNCS 11609, pp. 61–73, 2020.
https://doi.org/10.1007/978-3-030-51253-8_8

statements (possibly on the same channel), while the latter type sees one single agent making contradictory announcements on distinct channels. (In this second case, the agent announces something different from her beliefs.)

In this paper we only look at internal incoherences, within a multiple agent logical framework. The investigation of relational incoherence is left for further work.

Central topic of the present investigation being the set of possible communication attitudes of the agents. A communication attitude is the relation between reality facts and agent beliefs, or the relation between beliefs and announcements the agent makes. It is rather common that agents communicating on channels result not always to be competent on the matter they are talking about, or they can be insincere, or they can hide some (possibly private) information. The attitudes agents assume when communicating, or the ability to know true facts about the reality are important aspects of the communication processes. When we observe agents communicating, we typically have *prejudices* about their attitudes, where prejudices value an agent behaviour before observing what she announces.

There is a rather long research stream on the problem of aligning beliefs and announcements, that starts from Dynamic Epistemic Logic. (See [1], for a general framework analysis in the early stage of Public Announcement Logics (PAL), and recent development in [2–4].) Although these scholars have deeply dealt with the problem of announcements, they have made a very strong, and clearly oversimplified assumption: agents are always truthful and sincere. As a consequence, an observer on a communication channel always trusts the agents making announcements on that channel. In recent developments on PAL, the possibility that an announcement is made producing changes in beliefs of agents is provided in the form of belief revision operators: whenever an agent belief contrasts with what announced, she revises her knowledge base [4].

In this paper we investigate how to combine public announcements with beliefs that are also not necessarily aligned with the reality. Somebody can have a false belief or she can believe something that is not knows as true or false. Moreover agents can announce things they do not believe, or avoid to announce things they actually believe.

To clarify what we mean with the above introduced investigation definition, we provide a general example of announcements and their relations with truth and beliefs.

Example 1. Alice, Bob and Charlie travel quite often for work. They are also passionate about good food and they love visiting nice restaurants. To choose the best hotels and restaurants in town, they use as channels the social networks C_1 and C_2, where they are also active users by posting reviews and feedbacks. During their last business trip, they all stayed at the hotel H and they ate at the restaurants R_1, R_2 and R_3. Once back home, Bob posts a review on channel C_1 *announcing* that hotel H was dirty (saying $dirty(H)$), whilst on channel C_2 he announces that H was clean (saying $\neg dirty(H)$). Alice agrees with his announcement on C_1 but does not post any comment on C_2, while Charlie announces $\neg dirty(H)$ both on C_1 and C_2.

Assume that hotel H being clean or dirty is not a matter of opinions but a *provable* fact. It follows that we may draw some conclusions on the statements announced by Alice, Bob and Charlie on C_1 and C_2. First, Bob is not truthful since he announces $dirty(H)$ on C_1 and $\neg dirty(H)$ on C_2. It may be the case that he believes in only one of the two announces, and, consequently, he is lying in one of the two channels.

In this paper, we assume atemporal channels, so that when an agent observes a particular channel and contradicts herself in that channel the observer finds it out. Consequently we shall assume that agent make coherent announcements in every single channel, though it is possible that they make opposite announcements in distinct channels.

We assume *consistent* agents, that is agents that either believe in the truthfulness of a given statement, or believe in the truthfulness of the opposite statement; naturally, we allow that an agent may be not competent on a certain topic and, as such, believe in neither of them, but never to believe in both at the same. In the present paper, we shall focus our attention only on atemporal channels, leaving the study of temporal channels for further works. In temporal channels, an agent might announce a statement and, later, announce the opposite statement. Provided that she is not lying, this implies a belief revision process she passed through in order to change her way of thoughts.

Back to the example, while Bob and Charlie announce on every channel, Alice decides to express her opinions just on channel C_1.

Finally, Alice and Charlie are consistent with themselves even if not with one another. Therefore, they are both sincere but one of them is not competent. We shall assume that *competent* agents do *generally* know any topic discussed in every channel, while – admittedly a strong assumption – if the agent is ignorant in at least one topic, then she is considered incompetent. We are aware of the importance of this In this work, we shall deal with the problem of being competent on specific topics. Again, this topic is left for future research.

The rest of the paper is as follows. In Sect. 2 we define the logical language. In Sect. 3 we introduce the semantics of the logic and in Sect. 4 we provide a inference rules of the framework. Section 5 provides the prove of soundness for the introduced logic. We conclude the paper in Sect. 6 with a summary and a discussion of some related work and possible future work.

2 Multiple Channel Logic

In this section, we present our logical formalism, the *Multiple Channel Logic* (hereafter *MCL*); *MCL* is specified in terms of language.

MCL is a three-layered labelled, modal logical framework. The first layer of *MCL* is a propositional calculus. The second layer is a multi-modal calculus, where we can use three distinct modalities; notice that the three modalities are not dualised. Within the third layer, we habilitate *agent tagging* with the explicit purpose of allowing assertion of *prejudices* about agent communicative intentions, e.g., when we tag an agent to be sincere, or to be collaborative, and other positive or negative tags. The statement of an agent tag associated to a given agent is named a *prejudice*.

The general structure of *MCL* is typical of logical theories. An *MCL* theory is a triple $\langle \mathcal{W}, \mathcal{A}, \mathcal{R} \rangle$, where $\mathcal{W}$ is the logical language used to denote the theory, $\mathcal{A}$ is the set of axioms, and $\mathcal{R}$ is the set of inference rules, in our specific case, rewriting rules. When the set $\mathcal{A}$ is empty, then we call $\mathcal{T}$ a calculus. For a given *MCL*theory M we denote by $\mathcal{R}_M$ the set of axioms of M. To represent the set of rules $\mathcal{R}$, that is common to any *MCL* theory, we also use, for symmetry with $\mathcal{A}_M$ the notation $\mathcal{R}_M$.

We employ the alphabet

$$\sum = \mathcal{L} \cup C \cup \mathcal{M} \cup \mathcal{S} \cup \Lambda \cup \mathcal{T}$$

where:

$\mathcal{L}$ is a finite non-empty set of propositional letters $\mathcal{L} = \{A_1, A_2, \ldots, A_n\}$,
C is the set of connectives $C = \{\neg, \wedge, \vee \sim, -, \}$,
$\mathcal{M}$ is the set of modalities $\mathcal{M} = \{B, T_\square, T_\diamond\}$,
$\mathcal{S}$ is the set of logical signs $\mathcal{S} = \{(,), [,], \bot\}$,
Λ is a finite non-empty set of agents labels $\Lambda = \{\lambda_1, \ldots, \lambda_m\}$,
$\mathcal{T}$ is a finite non-empty set of agent tags $\mathcal{T} = \{Co, S, SCl, WCl, O\}$.

First, we introduce the notion of propositional formulae, that constitute the first layer of *MCL*Below, we provide the Backus-Naur Form definition of a propositional formula:

$$\varphi := A \mid \neg\varphi \mid \varphi \wedge \varphi \mid \varphi \vee \varphi$$

where A denotes a letter and formulae follow classic propositional logic format.

The second layer of *MCL* is a modal logic where the modal operators are B for beliefs, while $T_\square$ and $T_\diamond$ are the operators for the communication channels. We use $T_\square$ ($T_\diamond$) to recall the idea that an agent *tells* (*announces*) the embedded formula in every (at least one) communication channel. A modal formula is

$$\mu ::= B[\lambda : \varphi] \mid T_\square[\lambda : \varphi] \mid T_\diamond[\lambda : \varphi] \mid \sim\mu$$

where φ denotes a propositional formula. The modal formula for belief $B[\lambda : \varphi]$ is intended to denote that the agent λ believes φ. For the purpose of this paper, the intended notion of belief embeds the notion of knowledge as meant in Epistemic Logic.

The modal formula $T_\square[\lambda : \varphi]$ denotes that the agent λ announces φ in every channel. When, later on, we shall introduce its semantics, this notion will be further detailed, as related to the specific accessibility relation. In particular, we shall exhibit that a pair of channels is connected through the accessibility relation when observing the first channel implies observing the second one.

On the third layer of the logical framework we make use of the agent tags. An agent tag formula has one of the two formats

$$\alpha ::= +(X)\lambda \mid - (X)\lambda$$

where $X \in \{Co, S, SCl, WCl, O\}$ is an agent tag, and λ is the label representing the agent. The associated meaning attributed to the tags is as follows, where negative assertions with the $-$ sign are interpreted as the obvious negation:

$+(O)\lambda$ means that λ is *omniscient*,
$+(Co)\lambda$ means that λ is *competent*,
$+(S)\lambda$ means that λ is *sincere*,
$+(SCl)\lambda$ means that λ is *strongly collaborative*,
$+(WCl)\lambda$ means that λ is *weakly collaborative*.

3   The Semantics of *MCL*

In *MCL* the announcement of a formula by one agent cannot be bound to appear on a single, specific channel. We can only bind an announcement to appear in either all channels, or at least one. We therefore employ a semantics for the modalities that follows Kripke's modelling guidelines.

In order to build the semantics of a *MCL* theory we need to provide interpretation of the signature, first-layer formulae, second-layer formulae, agent tags.

Accordingly, the semantics of *MCL* is obtained as a tuple

$$\mathcal{M} = \langle \mathcal{W}_C, \mathcal{W}_{\mathcal{A}}, \mathcal{W}_{\mathcal{R}}, \mathcal{W}_{\mathcal{L}}, \mathcal{W}_{\mathcal{T}}, \mathcal{R}_C, \mathcal{I} \rangle$$

where:

- $\mathcal{W}_C$ is the domain of *Channels*, specified below;
- $\mathcal{W}_{\mathcal{A}}$ is the domain of *Agents*, specified below;
- $\mathcal{W}_{\mathcal{R}}$ is the domain of the *Reality*, i.e., the classic Boolean twofold interpretation domain $\{true, false\}$;
- $\mathcal{W}_{\mathcal{L}}$ is the domain of the *Letters*, a finite non-empty set, as numerous as the letters in the signature of *MCL*;
- $\mathcal{W}_{\mathcal{T}}$ is the domain of the *Tags*, a finite non-empty set as numerous as the agent tags in the signature of *MCL*;
- $\mathcal{R}_C$ is the accessibility relation between elements of $\mathcal{W}_C$;
- $\mathcal{I}$ is the *Interpretation* function.

Given a *MCL* theory M, that is not a pure language due to the set of axioms, we need to interpret the axioms into constraints to the world interpretations.

Every agent is associated to a world, which corresponds to a set of literals claimed to be true by that agent. The underlying idea is that an agent has a set of beliefs that can be mapped to true coherently with the classic interpretation of logic connectives and by assuming true those literals.

We assume that the accessibility relation is reflexive and transitive; $\mathcal{R}_C$ is neither assumed symmetric, nor antisymmetric.

Within our framework, we consider only *completely observable channels*, i.e., if an agent makes an announcement in one specific channel, then the theory allows the hypothetical observer to fully know that announcement in any case.

An interpretation of a *MCL M* is a *model* if, and only if:

- The interpretation of letters is a consistent propositional theory;
- The interpretation of each agent belief set is a consistent propositional theory;
- The set of announcements for each agent in every single channel is a consistent propositional theory;
- For every modal formula $T_\Box[\lambda : \varphi]$ asserted axiomatically in M and for every channel C in which φ is announced by λ, φ is announced by λ in every channel accessible from C;
- For every modal formula $T_\Diamond[\lambda : \varphi]$ asserted axiomatically in M and for every channel C in which φ is announced by λ, φ is announced by λ in at least one channel accessible from C;
- For every *omniscient* agent λ and every formula φ that is interpreted true in $\mathcal{W}_R$, then φ is also a belief of λ.
- For every *competent* agent λ and every formula φ believed by λ, then φ is interpreted true in $\mathcal{W}_R$.
- For every *sincere* agent, if a formula is announced in one channel, then its negation is not announced in another channel;
- For every *strongly collaborative* agent we find the announcement of every belief in every channel;
- For every *weakly collaborative* agent we find the announcement of every belief in at least one channel.

As usual, when a *MCL* theory M has a model, then M is called *satisfiable*. Conversely, when it has no model is called *unsatisfiable*. We assume that a set of axioms containing the symbol $\bot$ is always unsatisfiable.

4   A Deduction System for MCL

In this section we provide a set of inference rules for *MCL*. These rules are redundant, and we gather, as one of the further work issues, the provision of a minimised set of inference rules. In the stream of rules below, we prove some reducibilities of the rules, that are of special interest.

The rules can be of three distinct types:

- **Introduction rules** use the elements appearing in the antecedent for building those elements that appear in the subsequent;
- **Elimination rules** de-construct elements appearing in the antecedent into elements in the subsequent;
- $\bot$ **rules** introduce a contradiction, deriving $\bot$ in the subsequent.

The first group of rules, defined below, manage inference on the propositional layer of *MCL*, by means of inference rules. We adapted the classical presentation of Prawitz for propositional calculus to our needs. We shall then introduce a few other specific $\perp$ rules while providing the single contexts for the inference rules of the propositional layer, for the belief layer and finally for the announcement layer.

Without loss of generality we assume that axioms in a *MCL* theory M are all written in *Conjunctive Normal Form*, namely as conjunctions of disjiuctions of positive and negative literals. Rules of the propositional layer are classical deduction rules of Prawitz's presentation and are omitted here for the sake of space.

The second group of rules manage inference on the layer of beliefs. The group of rules R.7–R.12 mimic the basic rules of propositional logic in the Prawitz's presentation (left and right elimination of AND, Introduction of AND and OR, Introduction and elimination of double negation) and are omitted for the sake of space.

R.13 $\quad \dfrac{B[\lambda : \varphi]}{\sim B[\lambda : \neg\varphi]}$ [Coherence of disbeliefs]

As shown in many presentations of propositional calculus, as in Prawitz, we need rules that introduce $\perp$, as a means for shortening the process of inference. We provide the $\perp$ rules for the belief layer. The first rule is used for belief of contradiction, while the second rule is used for belief contradiction. A belief contradiction occurs when the claim of belief is contradicted by the claim of corresponding disbelief. We also have a belief contradiction rule corresponding to "Ex falso sequitur quodlibet in beliefs".

RC.3 $\quad \dfrac{B[\lambda : \varphi] \quad B[\lambda : (\neg\varphi)]}{\perp}$ [Belief of contradiction rule]

RC.4 $\quad \dfrac{B[\lambda : \perp]}{B[\lambda : \varphi]}$ [Belief "ex falso" rule]

RC.5 $\quad \dfrac{B[\lambda : \varphi] \quad \sim B[\lambda : \varphi]}{\perp}$ [Belief contradiction rule]

Finally we have the modus ponens rule for beliefs.

MP.2 $\quad \dfrac{B[\lambda : \varphi] \quad B[\lambda : \neg\varphi \vee \psi]}{\psi}$ [Belief modus ponens]

We obtain the clash in both situations where where we believe in φ and either we believe in the opposite, or (evidently) if we do not believe in it.

The third group of rules is introduced to manage inference on $T_\square$ and $T_\lozenge$ modalities. The first subgroup, formed by the rules R.12–R.16, supplies the five classical rules for introduction, left and right elimination for $\wedge$, introduction and elimination for double negation for $T_\square$. Rules from R.14 to R.19 are omitted for the sake of space, as they mimic rules R.7–R.13 already introduced for beliefs. Same holds for rules R-20–R-24, that mimic the same group of rules.

We now put forward a few basic rules that are needed for $T_\square$ and $T_\lozenge$ operators. First of all, we have a seriality rule for them, in rule R.23. We then have two rules for combined negations R.24 and R.25.

R.25 $\dfrac{T_\square[\lambda : \varphi]}{T_\Diamond[\lambda : \varphi]}$ [Seriality of $T_\square$ on $T_\Diamond$]

R.26 $\dfrac{T_\square[\lambda : \varphi]}{\sim T_\Diamond[\lambda : \neg\varphi]}$ [Coherence of missing announcements]

R.27 $\dfrac{T_\Diamond[\lambda : \varphi]}{\sim T_\square[\lambda : \neg\varphi]}$ [Coherence of provided announcements]

If agent λ announces φ on every channel, it is straightforward that she announces it on at least one channel (R.25). If λ announces φ on every channel, then in no channel she may announces the opposite (R.26). Lastly, if λ announces φ on at least one channel, then she cannot announce the opposite on every channel (R.27).

We now present the $\perp$ rules for announcements. Basically the contradictions consist in announcements of contradictions, and situations in which an agent announces everywhere a formula and announces somewhere its negation (an announcement contradiction).

RC.6 $\dfrac{T_\Diamond[\lambda : (\varphi \wedge \neg\varphi)]}{\perp}$ [Announcement contradiction on $T_\square$]

RC.7 $\dfrac{T_\square[\lambda : (\varphi \wedge \neg\varphi)]}{\perp}$ [Announcement of a contradiction]

RC.8 $\dfrac{T_\square[\lambda : \varphi] \quad T_\Diamond[\lambda : \neg\varphi]}{\perp}$ [Announcement contradiction on $T_\Diamond$]

RC.8 is the "son" of R.26–R.27: announcing φ on every channel clashes with announcing $\neg\varphi$ somewhere. Again we provide a modus ponens rule for $T_\square$ and $T_\Diamond$.

MP.3 $\dfrac{T_\square[\lambda : \varphi] \quad T_\Diamond[\neg\varphi \vee \psi]}{T_\Diamond : [\lambda : \psi]}$ [Channel universal modus ponens]

MP.4 $\dfrac{T_\Diamond[\lambda : \varphi] \quad T_\square[\neg\varphi \vee \psi]}{T_\Diamond : [\lambda : \psi]}$ [Channel universal modus ponens]

We need to manage introduction and elimination of missing beliefs and missing announces. We summarise the above by using the expression μ to denote a modal formula of *MCL*.

R.28 $\dfrac{\mu[\lambda : \varphi]}{\sim\sim \mu[\lambda : \varphi]}$ [Introduction of double $\sim$]

R.29 $\dfrac{\sim\sim \mu[\lambda : \varphi]}{\mu[\lambda : \varphi]}$ [Elimination of double $\sim$]

We are ready to introduce the rules for the agent tags. We have two rules that relate reality and beliefs, based on the expressed prejudice of omniscience and competence. Moreover, we have two pairs of rules for weak and strong collaboration tags, and one rule for sincereness which relates beliefs and communication channels.

All the above mentioned rules are employed for positive tags. For every positive tag, we have the dual rule for the negative counterpart.

R.30 $\dfrac{\varphi \quad + (O)\lambda}{B[\lambda : \varphi]}$ [Extension of $+(O)$]

R.31 $\dfrac{B[\lambda : \varphi] \quad + (Co)\lambda}{\varphi}$ [Extension of $+(Co)$]

R.32 $\dfrac{B[\lambda : \varphi] \quad + (Wcl)\lambda}{T_\diamond[\lambda : \varphi]}$ [Extension of $+(WCl)$]

R.33 $\dfrac{B[\lambda : \varphi] \quad + (SCl)\lambda}{T_\square[\lambda : \varphi]}$ [Extension of $+(SCl)$]

R.34 $\dfrac{T_\diamond[\lambda : \varphi] \quad + (S)\lambda}{B[\lambda : \varphi]}$ [Extension of $+(S)$]

R.35 $\dfrac{\sim B[\lambda : \varphi] \quad \varphi}{-(O)\lambda}$ [Introduction of $-(O)$]

R.36 $\dfrac{B[\lambda : \varphi] \quad \neg\varphi}{-(Co)\lambda}$ [Introduction of $-(Co)$]

R.37 $\dfrac{B[\lambda : \varphi] \quad \sim T_\diamond[\lambda : \varphi]}{-(Wcl)\lambda}$ [Introduction of $-(WCl)$]

R.39 $\dfrac{B[\lambda : \varphi] \quad \sim T_\square[\lambda : \varphi]}{-(Scl)\lambda}$ [Introduction of $-(SCl)$]

R.40 $\dfrac{T_\diamond[\lambda : \varphi] \quad \sim B[\lambda : \varphi]}{-(S)\lambda}$ [Introduction of $-(S)$]

An agent is esteemed omniscient if she knows every true formula. An agent is competent is every known formula is true. Notice that in the case of omniscience, the set of formulae believed true by the agent is a superset of the (actually) true formulae: the agent knows all what is true but she may also believe in some formulae proven neither true, nor false. On the contrary, in case of competence, the agent's beliefs are a subset of the true formulae; as such, all the agent's beliefs are proven to be true but there may be true formulae "out" of her knowledge base. Only when the agent knows all but true formulae the set of her beliefs and the set of true formulae are the same. If an agent believes that φ is true and she is weakly collaborative, then she will announces φ in at least one channel. Sincerity relates the communication of an agent with her beliefs. As such, a sincere agent that tells φ on a channel, then she believes φ to be true. We might be tempted to formulate sincerity from "the other agents' perspective" and state that occurs whenever an agent announces φ somewhere while $\neg\varphi$ anywhere. The proposed formulation of R.34 has the advantage that a sincere agent cannot contradict herself. This would lead to a contradiction due to λ being sincere and the application of R.34 to both $T_\diamond[\lambda : \varphi]$ and $T_\diamond[\lambda : \overline{\varphi}]$, and the subsequent application of RC.3.

Sincerity and collaboration do not derive one another. Assume three channels and that agent λ believes both formulae φ and ψ to be true. Suppose that λ announces φ on the first channel, $\neg\varphi$ on the second one, and ψ on the third one. In this setting, λ is collaborative but not sincere. Suppose now that λ solely announces ψ on the first channel. In this case, λ is sincere but not collaborative. It is straightforward to notice that R.33 subsumes R.32 through seriality. In addition, it implies a subtle form of sincerity. A strongly collaborative agent cannot announce anything she does believe to be true, even if she might announce something she believes to be neither true nor false. (Indeed, whenever the strongly collaborative λ has $\sim B\varphi$ as well as $\sim B\neg\varphi$, nothing prevent her to announce either φ or $\neg\varphi$ somewhere.)

Trivially, an agent: (R.35) is non-omniscient whenever she does not believe true an actually true formula, (R.36) is incompetent whenever she believe true a false formula. An agent is not weakly (strongly) collaborative if she knows something which she does not announce in at least one channel. Finally, an insincere agent announces, in at least one channel, a formula she does not believe to be true. In our formulation, it is not necessary that the agent believes in the truthfulness of a formula φ while announcing $\neg\varphi$ to be considered insincere.

R.36 depends on R.35. In fact, given the premises of R.35, by applying R.13 to $B[\lambda : \varphi]$ we obtain $\sim B[\lambda : \neg\varphi]$.

Finally we introduce the rules that provide contradictions between prejudices (positive and negative). The set of rules can be summarised by the expressions $+(P)\lambda$ as the assertion of the prejudice P on λ, and $-(P)\lambda$ as the negation of the prejudice P on λ.

RC.9 $\dfrac{+(P)\lambda \quad -(P)\lambda}{\perp}$ [Prejudice contradiction]

In order to manage the deduction process we need to provide a formal definition of the two types of conditions in which a deduction process can end. The set of the rules introduced above (introduction, elimination and $\perp$) form a set of rules that we henceforth name, for a theory M, the set $\mathcal{R}_M$

Proposition 1. $T_\square[\lambda : \varphi]$ and $T_\square[\lambda : \overline{\varphi}]$ provide a contradiction.

Proof. Trivial by application of R.12, R.21 and RC.4

Proposition 2. $T_\square[\lambda : (\varphi \wedge \neg\varphi)]$ provides a contradiction.

Proof. Trivial by application of R.21 and RC.4

5   Formal Properties of *MCL*

In this section we prove that *MCL* is sound with respect to the introduced semantics. The semantics cannot yet be proven to be complete.

The task we look at is *consistency checking*. Given a *MCL* theory M, we aim at establishing whether the set of axioms in M are consistent with each other, or, in other terms, whether they can or cannot derive a contradiction. The set of axioms in M are henceforth denoted by $\mathcal{A}_M$ and the set of rules of *MCL* is denoted by $\mathcal{R}_M$.

We assume that the axioms in the set $\mathcal{A}_M$, all formulae are written in Conjunctive Normal Form as already stated in Sect. 4. Given a *MCL* theory M, the set $\mathcal{A}_M^*$ is employed to denote the set of formulae that can be derived indirectly from $\mathcal{A}_M$ by applying the rules $\mathcal{R}_M$, in such a way that $\mathcal{A}_M^*$ is a *fixed point* for the transformation function derived by the application of the rules in $\mathcal{R}_M$. In other terms, the set $\mathcal{A}_M^*$ is derived by the rules applied to $\mathcal{A}_M$, and it is such that, by applying the rules again to it, the resulting transformed set is still $\mathcal{A}_M^*$. Since we are using clash rules, we have that, given a MCL theory M, where the set $\mathcal{A}_M^*$ contains $\bot$, then M is unsatisfiable. This is very simple to derive, If $\mathcal{A}_M^*$ contains $\bot$, then there can be two cases. Either $\mathcal{A}_M$ contains $\bot$, or it dos not. If it does not, then there is a specific transformation $\mathcal{A}_M^k$ of $\mathcal{A}_M$, that can be obtained by repeatedly applying the rules in $\mathcal{R}_M$ to $\mathcal{A}_M$, and there is the transformation $\mathcal{A}_M^*$ of $\mathcal{A}_M^k$ obtained by repeatedly applying the rules in $\mathcal{R}_M$ to $\mathcal{A}_M^k$ until no application of the rules results effective in transforming $\mathcal{A}_M^*$. The specificity of the transformation introduced above is that $\mathcal{A}_M^k$ has to contain at least one of the antecedents provided in rules $RC-1$ to $RC-9$. Those rules are all $\bot$ rules, and manage contradiction.

It is easy to prove the following intermediate result, that explains directly the approach we adopt to the problem of determining consistency, as well as to the problem of determining a model. Before to introduce Lemma 1, we need to introduce the notion of *purely disjunctive formula*. A purely disjunctive formula in MCL is either a propositional purely disjunctive formula, or a belief $B[\lambda : \varphi]$ whose propositional statement is a purely disjunctive formula, or a communication modal axiom $T_\Box[\lambda : \varphi]$ or $T_\Diamond[\lambda : \varphi]$ with the same constraint.

Given a finite set S of purely disjunctive formulae in MCL a choice of single literals occurring in each element of S is called a *combination* of S. In this case we mean that such a combination is consistently associated to the agents, for belief formulae, and to agents and a finite set of possible channels, whose minimum cardinality is one, and maximum cardinality is determined by the number of possible pairs formed by agents and statements announced in $\mathcal{A}_M^*$ by $T_\Diamond$. For instance, when three agents are named, and four announcements are made within the scope of $T_\Diamond$, the maximum number of possible channels is theoretically twelve, so that we can have the announcement of an agen for each of the formulae in each of the channels.

As in the premises of Tableaux techniques (see [5] as an introduction to methods of Tableaux for reasoning) we can prove the following lemma about models that can be derived from $\mathcal{A}_M^*$.

Lemma 1. *When $\mathcal{A}_M^*$ does not include $\bot$, then a consistent combination of purely disjunctive literals in $\mathcal{A}_M^*$ is a model of $\mathcal{A}_M$.*

Proof. Straightforwardly from rules $R.1-R.40$ and the fact that no rule $RC.1-RC.9$ has been applied, it would contain $\bot$). In detail, if all the formulae in $\mathcal{A}_M$ need to be satisfied, then we need to provide a consistent assignment of the literals appearing in $\mathcal{A}_M^*$ to satisfy the statements made by agents in $\mathcal{A}_M$. This is only possible if we find a consistent combination of purely disjunctive literals in $\mathcal{A}_M^*$, by the rules $R.1-R.29$. Rules $R.30-R.35$ only introduce elements that are rewritten by rules $R.1-R.29$. QED

Thanks to Lemma 1 we can introduce the extended notion of consistency to be used in MCL. A MCL theory M is consistent *iff* $\mathcal{A}_M^*$ derives a consistent combination of purely disjunctive literals.

A valid method for proving consistency of a MCL theory M is, therefore, to apply the rules to $\mathcal{A}_M$ until we obtain $\mathcal{A}_M^*$. When $\mathcal{A}_M^*$ does not contain $\perp$, we can look systematically at the combinations of literals obtained from $\mathcal{A}_M^*$, until we determine that one of those combination results consistent. At that point, we have found a model for $\mathcal{A}_M$. We can therefore derive the following theorem.

Theorem 1. *The rules of* MCL *are sound.*

6   Related and Further Works

In this paper we dealt with the problem of combining beliefs and announcements in a framework that also allows to provide prejudices about agent communication attitudes. The basic results we obtained are: (i.) a formalisation of the modal logic MCL which allows to express facts, beliefs and announcements, (ii.) the analysis of a semantics for this logic, and (iii.) the proof of soundness for the logic itself.

As stated in Sect. 1, we have based our work on the stream of extensions to Dynamic Epistemic Logic, in particular referring to PAL, which was originally proposed by Plaza in [6]. The basis of our approach has been to quit the oversimplified assumption of truthfulness of agents. Issues about truthfulness of agents have often been dealt with in PAL and other agent-based logic approaches, as in [7].

In [8], the authors dealt with the problem of how to express a semantics for Agent Communication Logic in order to make non-monotonic inferences on the ground of speech acts. The above mentioned researches have exploited the flaws we referred to in this paper. Some attempts to solve these flaws have been proposed in many further studies.

Although interesting perspectives, the focus of those papers and their aims share little with the purpose of this work. To complete this short analysis of the reference literature, an important investigation regards complexity of reasoning in PAL. In [9], the author proves two interesting results: Satisfiability in single-agent PAL is NP-complete and in multi-agent PAL is PSpace-complete.

This work has been based on the schema of layered logic approach as used for meaning negotiation, risk analysis and energy management by Cristani et al. [10–14].

There are several ways in which this research can be taken further. First, we shall investigate completeness of MCL. Moreover, we are developing a tableaux approach to the consistency checking, essentially by extending the method used for proving soundness in this paper. We are finally looking at extensions to the logical framework to cover *partially observable channels* that include temporal aspects and access permissions. Agent tags presented in Sect. 4 might be refined. For instance, an agent can be considered insincere only when announcing the opposite of a belief of hers, while an agent making a statement on which she has no knowledge of truthfulness might be classified as braggart.

References

1. van Benthem, J., van Eijck, J., Kooi, B.P.: Logics of communication and change. Inf. Comput. **204**(11), 1620–1662 (2006)
2. Balbiani, P., Guiraud, N., Herzig, A., Lorini, E.: Agents that speak: modelling communicative plans and information sources in a logic of announcements. In: 10th International Conference on Autonomous Agents and Multiagent Systems (AAMAS 2011), Taipei, Taiwan, 2–6 May 2011, vol. 1–3, pp. 1207–1208 (2011)
3. Sonenberg, L., Stone, P., Tumer, K., Yolum, P. (eds.) 10th International Conference on Autonomous Agents and Multiagent Systems (AAMAS 2011), Taipei, Taiwan, 2–6 May 2011, vol. 1–3. IFAAMAS (2011)
4. Balbiani, P., Seban, P.: Reasoning about permitted announcements. J. Philos. Logic **40**(4), 445–472 (2011). https://doi.org/10.1007/s10992-011-9187-1
5. Olivetti, N. (ed.): TABLEAUX 2007. LNCS (LNAI), vol. 4548. Springer, Heidelberg (2007). https://doi.org/10.1007/978-3-540-73099-6
6. Plaza, J.: Logics of public communications. Synthese **158**(2), 165–179 (2007)
7. Wooldridge, M.: Semantic issues in the verification of agent communication languages. Auton. Agents Multi-Agent Syst. **3**(1), 9–31 (2000). https://doi.org/10.1023/A:1010090027213
8. Boella, G., Governatori, G., Hulstijn, J., Riveret, R., Rotolo, A., van der Torre, L.: Time and defeasibility in FIPA ACL semantics. J. Appl. Logic **9**(4), 274–288 (2011)
9. Lutz, C.: Complexity and succinctness of public announcement logic. In: 5th International Joint Conference on Autonomous Agents and Multiagent Systems (AAMAS 2006), Hakodate, Japan, 8–12 May 2006, pp. 137–143 (2006)
10. Cristani, M., Tomazzoli, C., Karafili, E., Olivieri, F.: Defeasible reasoning about electric consumptions, vol. 2016, pp. 885–892, May 2016
11. Burato, E., Cristani, M.: The process of reaching agreement in meaning negotiation. In: Nguyen, N.T. (ed.) Transactions on Computational Collective Intelligence VII. LNCS, vol. 7270, pp. 1–42. Springer, Heidelberg (2012). https://doi.org/10.1007/978-3-642-32066-8_1
12. Tomazzoli, C., Cristani, M., Karafili, E., Olivieri, F.: Non-monotonic reasoning rules for energy efficiency. J. Ambient Intelligence Smart Environ. **9**(3), 345–360 (2017)
13. Burato, E., Cristani, M.: Learning as meaning negotiation: a model based on English auction. In: Håkansson, A., Nguyen, N.T., Hartung, R.L., Howlett, R.J., Jain, L.C. (eds.) KES-AMSTA 2009. LNCS (LNAI), vol. 5559, pp. 60–69. Springer, Heidelberg (2009). https://doi.org/10.1007/978-3-642-01665-3_7
14. Cristani, M., Karafili, E., Viganò, L.: Tableau systems for reasoning about risk. J. Ambient Intell. Humaniz. Comput. **5**(2), 215–247 (2013). https://doi.org/10.1007/s12652-013-0186-7

Dataset Anonyization on Cloud: Open Problems and Perspectives

Matteo Cristani[✉] and Claudio Tomazzoli

Department of Computer Science, University of Verona, Verona, Italy
matteo.cristani@univr.it

Abstract. Data anonymization is the process of making information contained in a group of data such that it is not possible to identify unique references to single elements in the group after the process. This action, when conducted onto datasets used to make statistical inference is bound to have ananlogous behaviours on certain indices before and after the process itself. In this paper we study the pipeline of anonymization process for datasets, when this pipeline is managed on cloud technology, where cryptography is not applicable at all, for datasets being available in an open setting. We examine the open problems, and devise a method to address these problems in a logical framework.

In this study we aim at defining a method for dataset anonymization based on logic paradigm. This approach is able to address some open problems in data anonymization, that are left yet unsolved in the current literature, and provides a general framework for the identification of parameters to be used to establish the perimeter of anonymization of datasets.

The anonymization problem can be described as follows. Consider a dataset D, that contains two groups of columns (C' and C'') distinguished as *anagraphic* and *rough data*. We consider a raw r in the dataset to be *disclosed* when it is communicated in some modified form to a subject s, who is not authorized to treat the anagraphic data, and there is a way for s to identify the anagraphic columns of r. The dataset may be equipped with *provenance data*, namely information regarding the context in which the data have been extracted. This provenance information generally consists in a further dataset P where you have the anagraphic data (and not all the rough, and possibly other rough ones) of a larger set, such that the distinct raws of D that contain only the anagraphic data are a subset of P.

The problem of data anonymization is partly dissimilar to the problem of privacy. We need to preserve the privacy of the data, but simultaneously we wish to communicate entirely the dataset to someone who should not be able to disclose the identity in those data, that can be associated to the raws.

The simplest process of anonymization consists in eliminating the anagraphic data, and generate a new dataset, where only the rough data are exposed. This action has a number of drawbacks that suggest not to use it:

- The dataset can lack unique pointers to raws;

M. Brambilla et al. (Eds.): ICWE 2019 Workshops, LNCS 11609, pp. 74–85, 2020.
https://doi.org/10.1007/978-3-030-51253-8_9

- The correlations between anagraphic and rough data are lost;
- Nevertheless, it might still be possible to leak anagraphic data thanks to other provenance information.

The last point is decisive to instantiate the approach we propose here. When we are able to distinguish data (and possibly identify them) within the dataset after anonymization, the anonymization process is not finalized, ad it is still possible to leak anagraphic data, as shown in the following example.

Example 1. Consider a dataset D that contains data of the directive personnel of a company, consisting in name, surname, role and age of each person. We consider anagraphic name and surname, whilst role and age are rough. We have provenance information in the form of a dataset with name, surname and age. In the anonymised dataset, where the data preservation of the rough data is total, and the anagrphic data are cancelled, we only have ages. Assume that in one raw of the provenance we have that one age results unique. Thus, the raw in the dataset can be attached with the name and surname of the person.

There is a newly valuable paradigm of data management that generates a specific question regarding data anonymization: the cloud. The nature of this process is determined by the need to collaborate in data analysis, where the motivation to collaborate is in tradeoff with the need of preserving data anonimity. This is specifically the case of enterprise data. When a cloud service for knowledge discovery from data is offered to the public, it is often stated that the risk for the company is sharing the data is limited if not null, under the consideration that the data provenance is masked by data anonymization. In this context, data provenance (see [1–3] for recent references) is not a technique to test trustworthiness or guarantee authenticity, but, on the opposite, an attack to privacy.

The formalization of the problem in logical terms gives account to some novel issues. In particular we shall identify three formal problems that are still unsolved, and settle them in logical terms.

The rest of the paper is organised as follows. Section 1 discusses the dataset anonymization process and provides an analysis of the open problems in the process pipeline, Sect. 2 shows that the nature of the dataset anonymization is essentially equivalent to the problem of preserving certain logic properties of an induction process. In Sect. 3 we show an example of application of the method and discuss the open problems. Section 4 discusses related and future work and finally Sect. 5 takes some conclusions.

1   Data Pipeline in Data Anonymization Processes

To help providing a general view of the concept of data anonymization, we provide here an analysis of the acquired knowledge on the topic, that is mainly centered in the notion of *pipeline* of the process itself. Some of the steps are performed by means of different methods, some are included only when one specific

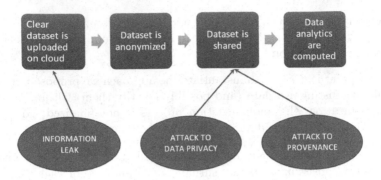

Fig. 1. The dataset anonymization pipeline.

method is proposed. The dataset anonymization process we aim at defining is described in Fig. 1.

In particular, the process of uploading a dataset on the cloud is generally considered safe, so we document the risk in terms of classic information leak, due to the weakness of the privacy method employed to protect data during the upload process. Once we have anonymized the dataset on the cloud, we assume that the dataset is not anymore protected. This is the case, for instance, of a cloud platform for scientific experiments, where data with delicate privacy properties attached, such as health data (the most common example of datasets on which privacy preserving anonymization processes are performed), but again we need the scientific community to be able to address those datasets for experiment validation or experiment data extensions. Another case that is very interesting is the one of commercial or anyhow sensitive business data. There is a strong interest of companies in having data of concurrency and data of actors in the same market shared, in order to fine tune business policies. However, there is an obvious skepticism of the companies in doing this for the intrinsic risk of being attacked on the data anonimity. On the one hand, for the obligation to keep privacy on those data due to national or international laws, such as GDPR in the European Union, and on the other hand for the risk of being attacked on data provenance, where relevant private data can be used to mark weakness of concurrency.

A research question becomes: is it possible to preserve both privacy of individual data and provenance with some form of anonymization?

At first, we need a general definition of *anonymization*. The basic notion is the one of dataset, that need to be treated in a formal way. What we aim at is providing a definition that can fit a logical framework. The closest notion of dataset that satisfies this requirement is the one of *A-box* in Description Logic, that in turn is a simplified version of *ground unquantified theory* in First Order Logic, or at another level, the notion of *Fact set* in nonmonotonic frameworks, or a set of ground formulae in *Logic programming*. To simplify the notion, we assume a logical apparatus of first order ground expressiveness *à la Prolog* where the logic programming setup is determined by first order clauses with negation interpreted as failure, conjunction and negation. Definition are assumed as interpreting implications between formulae and simple formulae with variables. Ground formulae are simplified to be pure predicative assertions.

Summarizing:

- **A definition:** $p(x_1, x_2, \ldots, x_n)$:- $expr$;
- **An expression:** $-expr$ or $expr_1, expr_2, \ldots, expr_m$ or $expr_1; expr_2, \ldots, expr_m$;
- **A constant/variable:** c not in the set of variables x;
- **A ground formula:** $p(c_1, c_2, \ldots, c_n)$ with c_i constant.

A set of ground formulae is named a *dataset*, and a set of pure definitions is named a *scheme*. A dataset D is said to *refer* to a scheme S when the predicates used in the dataset are all defined in the scheme.

We name analytical property of a dataset D one of the following measures[1]:

- **Count**, the operation of counting the elements of D that satisfy a given formula ϕ. In particular **Count**$(\phi, \mathbf{D}, \mathbf{S})$ is the number of constants in D such that $D \cup S \vDash \phi(c)$;
- **Avg**, the operation of computing the average value of the elements that satisfy a given formula;
- **Min**, the operation of computing the minimal value of the elements that satisfy a given formula;
- **Max**, the operation of computing the maximal value of the elements that satisfy a given formula;
- **Percent**, the operation of computing the percentile value as specified. In particular **Percent**$(\phi, \mathbf{p}, \mathbf{D}, \mathbf{S})$ is the value of the p percentile of the distribution of the elements of D that satisfy ϕ. Specifically, **Percent**$(\phi, \mathbf{50}, \mathbf{D}, \mathbf{S})$ is the median.
- **Stddev**, the standard deviation of the elements satisfying a given formula.
- **Corr**, the operation of computing the correlation index of the elements satisfying a given pair of formulae. Therefore, **Corr**$(\phi, \psi, \mathbf{D}, \mathbf{S})$ is the correlation index of the elements in D that satisfy ϕ and ψ.
- **Regr**, as above but with the regression index.

We name *identification criterion* a function χ that takes in input the constants appearing in a dataset D and maps them onto a set of values in a set V named the *provenance set*.

Definition 1. *Given a dataset D based on a scheme S, a set of analytical properties P of the predicates in D, and a provenance set V, we define the* Basic dataset anonymization problem, *the problem of finding a dataset D', based on the same scheme S, enjoying the same properties P and such that for any constant c appearing in D, and for any applicable identification criterion χ, even if $\chi(D, c)$ is defined, $\chi(D', c)$ is however undefined.*

---

[1] We introduce here the notion of analytical properties in terms of statistical measures, the most common properties desired in dataset anonymization.

As formulated above, we can also provide the definition of cases in which the anonymization problem cannot be solved, as it might not be possible to compute a dataset D' with the desired properties, that simultaneously satisfies the anonymization desiderata. By weakening the request with thresholds on the analytics we have the following.

Definition 2. *Given a dataset D based on a scheme S, a set of analytical properties $P = \{p_1, p_2, \ldots, p_n\}$ of the predicates in D, each associated with a thresholds τ_i, a provenance set V, we define the* Dataset anonymization problem on thresholded parameters, *the problem of finding a dataset D', based on the same scheme S, enjoying the properties of P within the thresholds as defined above, and such that for any constant c appearing in D, and for any applicable identification criterion χ, even if $\chi(D, c)$ is defined, $\chi(D', c)$ is however undefined.*

We can extend the above by means of a reduction of the request on the identification within a threshold.

Definition 3. *Given a dataset D based on a scheme S, a set of analytical properties P of the predicates in D, and a provenance set V, we define the* Dataset thresholded anonymization problem, *the problem of finding a dataset D', based on the same scheme S, enjoying the same properties P and such that for at least τ constants c appearing in D, and for any applicable identification criterion χ, even if $\chi(D, c)$ is defined, $\chi(D', c)$ is however undefined.*

The combined version of the above is:

Definition 4. *Given a dataset D based on a scheme S, a set of analytical properties $P = \{p_1, p_2, \ldots, p_n\}$ of the predicates in D, each associated with a thresholds τ_i, a provenance set V, we define the* Generalized dataset anonymization problem, *the problem of finding a dataset D', based on the same scheme S, enjoying the properties of P within the thresholds as defined above, and such that for at least τ constants c appearing in D, and for any applicable identification criterion χ, even if $\chi(D, c)$ is defined, $\chi(D', c)$ is however undefined.*

We assume here that the thresholds can be given, with a slight abuse of notation, in form of percentage or percentile on the analytics and on the criteria.

2   Inductive Rules and Data Anonymization

We shall not get onto the details of current methods of Inductive Logic Programming, as used in dataset analysis. We specifically consider the approaches that generate theories satisfying one condition of derivability of the theory itself starting from the dataset onto the theory and back, as discussed in some recent approaches [4,5].

The ideal loop would be:

- The dataset D is the application base of an algorithm of ILP that generates a scheme S, such that D is entirely dependent on S as studied in many investigations, for instance [6–8];
- The scheme and the dataset form a theory that is the most general possible one, able to derive D and being as small as possible.

There can be variants of the above schematic method. On the one hand, we might be interested in accepting theories that are not able to derive the entire dataset, allowing for *exceptions*. This drives to the development of nonmonotonic ILP frameworks [9–12].

Clearly, at the end of the above process, we still have the dataset D in hands. However, the logic program obtained so far has more than one possible datasets that are compatible, or better, that can substitute D. In particular, we can only consider the scheme S, and provide a novel dataset D', compatible with S that we aim at guaranteeing the same properties but after anonymization. We essentially need to iterate the ILP above defined schema until a predefined set of possible datasets is computed that satisfy the requested properties and is anonymized.

The challenge is not trivial, as the number of possible datasets is infinite, a priori, and therefore, we either have a method to restrict the admissible datasets, or we have a method to establish that a correct database is not available. A very simple, yet general, algorithmic approach, is defined in Algorithm 1.

Data: A dataset D, a set of properties P a provenance set V
Result: A dataset D' with the same properties P such that provenance
         of elements in D cannot be detected
Generates by ILP the initial scheme S of D;
while *Provenance is not hidden* **do**
    while *Properties are not satisfied* **do**
        Generates new dataset D';
        if D' *does not satisfy* P **then**
            | set Properties not satisfied;
        end
    end
    if D' *does not hide provenance* V **then**
        | Generates new dataset D';
    end
end

Algorithm 1. BILP: Basic iterative ILP schema for dataset control in dataset anonymization problem.

When the computation of ILP scheme is driven by up-to-date methods we know that completeness of the combinatorics can be guaranteed as the Inverse Entailment problem is dealt with approaches that prevent incompleteness in the hypotheses search. However, this is not sufficient to determine completeness of the schema, when applied to datasets, and aiming at preserving provenance protection and properties preservation.

If we aim at preserving **Count**, and the domains of all the predicates is finite we can prove Observation 1.

Observation 1. *Algorithm **BILP** finitely iterates on admissible schemes and computes a finite number of acceptable datasets when the ILP algorithm is complete on hypotheses search, the requested properties are only **Count** and the domains of predicates appearing in the input dataset are constrained to finite sets.*

The nature of this finite iterations depends on the preservation needs, that are going to be analysed in Sect. 3 for the other requirements. In particular average, percentiles and standard deviation alone cannot guarantee finite solvability. The Algorithm, in fact, might require an infinite number of steps to be performed, in the general case. The decidability of the four problems defined in Sect. 1 needs to be addressed (and this shall be matter of future work). Following the line of complexity issues, we also need to determine complexity of the algorithm in the finite domain case, and possibly lower bound to the complexity of the problem itself.

On the other hand, perfect convergence with constraints onto numerical values may simply be impossible.

Observation 2. *Algorithm **BILP** can infinitely iterate on admissible schemes and compute an infinite number of acceptable datasets when the ILP algorithm is complete on hypotheses search, if the requested properties are **Avg** or **Stddev**.*

Finally, we need to compare the algorithm performance with other options in the decision process. For instance, theory syntesis may be performed by techniques of Association Rules, instead that with ILP, and the very same ILP method can be performing differently when different methods are applied.

3 An Example of the Deduction Process as Anonymization Task

The deduction process can be completely different for Algorithm **BILP**, depending on the properties that we need to preserve. In this section we show, by some simplified examples, how the proposed method works. First of all, we introduce the sample data of Table 1.

Table 1. Sample data.

Name	Age	Gender	Income	Position
Frank	53	M	56000	Administrative senior manager
George	42	M	51000	Salesperson
Emily	38	F	64000	HR executive
Andrew	50	M	59000	Production director
John	56	M	66000	Sales senior manager
Mary	29	F	86000	CFO
Bob	33	M	46000	Technical consultant
Alice	28	F	32000	Secretariat
Albert	63	M	95000	CEO
Jane	52	F	41000	Salesperson

The provenance information is mapped as follows:

Frank	Frank Marble	TheCompany ltd	
George	George Anders	Private	
Emily	Emily Birken	TheCompany ltd	HR Executive
Andrew	Andrew Borg	TheCompany ltd	
John	John Smith	TheCompany ltd	
Mary	Mary Hill	TheCompany ltd	CFO
Bob	Robert Kiel	TheConsultants ltd	
Alice	Alice Perp	TheCompany ltd	
Albert	Albert Frank	TheCompany ltd	CEO
Jane	Jane Jill	Private	

We assume that the analytic data are **Count**, **Avg** on income and **Stddev** on income on total, male and female employees and collaborators and distinctively between sales and other employees.

The summary of the analytics made in clear is on Table 2.

Table 2. Analytic results.

Operation	Restriction	Value
Count	Total	10
Count	Male	6
Count	Female	4
Count	Sales	3
Count	Non-sales	7

(contniued)

Table 2. *(contniued)*

Avg	Total	59600
Avg	Male	62166
Avg	Female	55750
Avg	Sales	52666
Avg	Non-sales	62571
Stddev	Total	18413
Stddev	Male	15952
Stddev	Female	21004
Stddev	Sales	10274
Stddev	Non-sales	20240

While running ILP algorithms, we may expect many different results, depending on the actual mapping provided in the table. Assuming that the single values are indeed employed for the computation of the data represented in logical terms, we may have a representation, exemplified for the first raw in the original dataset:

- Name(ID_1, Frank);
- Age(ID_1, 53);
- Gender(ID_1, M);
- Income(ID_1, 56000);
- Position(ID_1, Administrative senior manager);

Assuming a namespace for person names, ages, genders, and positions that result acceptable for this process, we may generate by ILP some rules that cover the distribution of values on incomes (the value on which analytics are performed indeed). The resulting anonymization can vary in terms of elements, but depends entirely upon the setup of the namespaces. For instance, age is quite easily established in terms of the integer interval [0..120], but the need to preserve average and standard deviation may lead to a significant restriction of the variants. Same thing happens for the domain of incomes, that may be a range [0..200000], for instance. Again, the need for a control upon average and standard deviation can lead to limited variants.

A possible conversion of the table is presented in Table 3.

It is easy to see that the result is almost perfect for age and the total average and standard deviation. However, the average income of female employees is 52500, neatly less than the original dataset. In other terms, if the above would be the result of one computation by the deductive process at the end of the induction performed with **BILP** method, this would not be acceptable and a further execution of the inner cycle would be needed.

On the other hand, many discoveries can be directly made about the data provenance, in the resulting dataset. In particular, **Tim** can be immediately identified as Albert Frank, **Henriette** as Emily Birken and **Hope** as Mary Hill.

Table 3. Sample data.

Name	Age	Gender	Income	Position
Jim	28	M	39000	Administrative senior manager
Adam	30	M	34000	Salesperson
Henriette	28	F	80000	HR executive
Al	55	M	57000	Production director
Jo	52	M	55000	Sales senior manager
Hope	49	F	66000	CFO
Albert	38	M	47000	Technical consultant
Giselle	53	F	60000	Secretariat
Tim	59	M	57000	CEO
Jackie	52	F	101000	Salesperson

Out of this, notice that **Adam** and **Jackie** can be identified as George Anders and Jane Jill, respectively, being one male and one female Salespersons. At this end, we also know that **Giselle** is Alice Perp, **Al** is Andrew Borg, and so on.

To prevent the leak of this information pieces, we need to force stronger anonymization steps, possibly to conclude that the anonymization is impossible for that dataset.

4   Related Work

In this study we have been dealing with the combination of two basic methods: inductive logic programming and data anonymization. In particular, relatively to data anonymization, we have been dealing with the problems of making constraints to privacy trade off the constraints to statistical patterns preservation.

To better focus the complexity of the nature of the problem, we should observe that many issues of data anonymization that are unsolved at this stage, regard the anonymization of *unstructured data*, in particular data containing text. Consider for instance the problem of anonyization of the data field **Position** as illustrated in Sect. 3. Since this was requested, we did not anonymize the positions, for one of the requested queries under which we need to provide correct restriction was indeed the distinction between sales and non-sales. In any case, the anonymization process should be driven by a dictionary. We illustrated in the example an anonymization step for the field **Name** that took elements in the dictionary of names. This should be guaranteed against attacks based on co-occurrence and direct knowledge extraction from text [13–15].

Authors have already made use of non-monotonic techniques for reasoning about energy [16]. That work was partly based on studies on nonmonotonic preferences [17–19] and partly on work on meaning negotiation [20, 21]. In further studies we shall develop henceforth, we aim at defining a framework that develops meaning negotiation techniques for data anonymization based on ILP.

5   Conclusions

This preliminary investigation had two major aims:

- Devising a methodology for incorporating ILP techniques and Statistical Natural Language Processing methods in the process of Data Anonymization;
- Identifying open problems of Data Anonymization that are related to the above approach, for which a further investigation based on the sketched approach is worth.

We have identified four open problems, that are probabilistic variants of the basic one: making impossible to detect the provenance of data whilst preserving their statistical patterns against relevant queries. Once such a problem is addressed we can construct a cloud-based system that can be used to share data of private provenance, without disclosing the privacy, but having the opportunity of using the statistical patterns for specific purposes, such as market survey or social network analysis.

An immediate development of the problem is to guarantee the privacy of the provenance even when the data are shared (or better, after the sharing process), when the data are compared to other data groups, and it is possible to generate a leak of a different nature than the one caused by the disclosure of provenance per se. For instance, when a data group is uploaded on cloud and the provenance is not revealed, we may obtain provenance data, indirectly, by comparing those data with data groups of others that we understand are competitors. If we know, for instance, that the data group 1 and data group 2 are data of companies a and b, but do not know which one is a and b we can derive this by comparative data. Therefore we might also be interested in processes of *partial masking* where data can be revealed to subsets of the potential users.

References

1. Simmhan, Y., Plale, B., Gannon, D.: A survey of data provenance in e-science. SIGMOD Rec. **34**(3), 31–36 (2005)
2. Buneman, P., Khanna, S., Wang-Chiew, T.: Why and where: a characterization of data provenance. In: Van den Bussche, J., Vianu, V. (eds.) ICDT 2001. LNCS, vol. 1973, pp. 316–330. Springer, Heidelberg (2001). https://doi.org/10.1007/3-540-44503-X_20
3. Buneman, P., Khanna, S., Tan, W.-C.: Data provenance: some basic issues. In: Kapoor, S., Prasad, S. (eds.) FSTTCS 2000. LNCS, vol. 1974, pp. 87–93. Springer, Heidelberg (2000). https://doi.org/10.1007/3-540-44450-5_6
4. Lima, R., Espinasse, B., Freitas, F.: A logic-based relational learning approach to relation extraction: the ontoilper system. Eng. Appl. Artif. Intell. **78**, 142–157 (2019)
5. Kazmi, M., Schueller, P., Saygin, Y.: Improving scalability of inductive logic programming via pruning and best-effort optimisation. Expert Syst. Appl. **87**, 291–303 (2017)

6. Lisi, F., Malerba, D.: Inducing multi-level association rules from multiple relations. Mach. Learn. **55**(2), 175–210 (2004)
7. Lisi, F.: Building rules on top of ontologies for the semantic web with inductive logic programming. Theory Pract. Log. Program. **8**(3), 271–300 (2008)
8. Lisi, F.: Inductive logic programming in databases: From datalog to dl+log. Theory Pract. Log. Program. **10**(3), 331–359 (2010)
9. Ray, O.: Nonmonotonic abductive inductive learning. J. Appl. Log. **7**(3), 329–340 (2009)
10. Sakama, C.: Induction from answer sets in nonmonotonic logic programs. ACM Trans. Comput. Log. **6**(2), 203–231 (2005)
11. Sakama, C., Inoue, K.: Brave induction: a logical framework for learning from incomplete information. Mach. Learn. **76**(1), 3–35 (2009)
12. Sakama, C.: Nonmonotomic inductive logic programming. In: Eiter, T., Faber, W., Truszczyński, M. (eds.) LPNMR 2001. LNCS (LNAI), vol. 2173, pp. 62–80. Springer, Heidelberg (2001). https://doi.org/10.1007/3-540-45402-0_5
13. Zorzi, M., Combi, C., Lora, R., Pagliarini, M., Moretti, U.: Automagically encoding adverse drug reactions in MedDRA, pp. 90–99 (2015). [26]
14. Zorzi, M., Combi, C., Pozzani, G., Arzenton, E., Moretti, U.: A co-occurrence based MedDRA terminology generation: some preliminary results. In: ten Teije, A., Popow, C., Holmes, J.H., Sacchi, L. (eds.) AIME 2017. LNCS (LNAI), vol. 10259, pp. 215–220. Springer, Cham (2017). https://doi.org/10.1007/978-3-319-59758-4_24
15. Zorzi, M., Combi, C., Pozzani, G., Moretti, U.: Mapping free text into MedDRA by natural language processing: a modular approach in designing and evaluating software extensions, pp. 27–35 (2017). [28]
16. Tomazzoli, C., Cristani, M., Karafili, E., Olivieri, F.: Non-monotonic reasoning rules for energy efficiency. J. Ambient Intell. Smart Environ. **9**(3), 345–360 (2017)
17. Governatori, G., Olivieri, F., Rotolo, A., Scannapieco, S., Cristani, M.: Picking up the best goal an analytical study in defeasible logic. In: Morgenstern, L., Stefaneas, P., Lévy, F., Wyner, A., Paschke, A. (eds.) RuleML 2013. LNCS, vol. 8035, pp. 99–113. Springer, Heidelberg (2013). https://doi.org/10.1007/978-3-642-39617-5_12
18. Governatori, G., Olivieri, F., Scannapieco, S., Cristani, M.: Superiority based revision of defeasible theories. In: Dean, M., Hall, J., Rotolo, A., Tabet, S. (eds.) RuleML 2010. LNCS, vol. 6403, pp. 104–118. Springer, Heidelberg (2010). https://doi.org/10.1007/978-3-642-16289-3_10
19. Cristani, M., Tomazzoli, C., Karafili, E., Olivieri, F.: Defeasible reasoning about electric consumptions, pp. 885–892 (May 2016)
20. Burato, E., Cristani, M.: The process of reaching agreement in meaning negotiation. In: Nguyen, N.T. (ed.) Transactions on Computational Collective Intelligence VII. LNCS, vol. 7270, pp. 1–42. Springer, Heidelberg (2012). https://doi.org/10.1007/978-3-642-32066-8_1
21. Burato, E., Cristani, M., Viganò, L.: A deduction system for meaning negotiation. In: Omicini, A., Sardina, S., Vasconcelos, W. (eds.) DALT 2010. LNCS (LNAI), vol. 6619, pp. 78–95. Springer, Heidelberg (2011). https://doi.org/10.1007/978-3-642-20715-0_5

Second International Workshop on Maturity of Web Engineering Practices (MATWEP 2019)

Second International Workshop on Maturity of Web Engineering Practices (MATWEP 2019)

José González Enríquez[1], Francisco José Domínguez Mayo[1], Nora Koch[2], and Esteban Morillo Baro[3]

[1] University of Seville
jgenriquez@us.es
fjdominguez@us.es
[2] IWT2 Group, University of Seville
nora.koch@iwt2.org
[3] Servinform, S.A., Spain
emorillob@servinform.es

Abstract. Knowledge transfer and adoption of software engineering approaches by practitioners is always a challenge for both, academia and industry. The objective of the workshop MATWEP is to provide an open discussion space that combines solid theory work with practical on-the-field experience in the Web Engineering area. The topics covered are knowledge transfer of Web Engineering approaches, such as methods, techniques and tools in all phases of the development lifecycle of Web applications. We report on the papers presented in the edition 2019 and the fruitful discussion on these topics.

Keywords: Web engineering · Knowledge transfer · Industrial environment

1 Introduction and Motivation

The second International Workshop on Maturity of Web Engineering Practices (MATWEP 2019) was held in conjunction with the 19th International Conference on Web Engineering (ICWE 2019) in Daejeon (Korea) on June 11th, 2019. The motivation of this initiative stands in the aim of building a better bridge from the theory to the practice; from academia to industry.

The focus of this second workshop and future editions of MATWEP are the analysis and discussion on positive experiences and difficulties that arise in the construction of such bridges. The goal is to show the lessons learned in the knowledge transfer process. This way it promotes to obtain feedback from practitioners for improving Web Engineering techniques, methods and approaches developed in research-intensive environments.

2 Presentations and Discussion

During the second edition of the workshop five papers have been selected for presentations at the workshop; two of them have been selected to be published in these proceedings. We hope you find these papers useful reading material.

The first paper written by Gefei Zhang and Jianjun Zhao presents a white-box method for separating user interactions from each other. Thanks to the separated interactions, the method proposed by the authors helps to achieve a better understanding the control and data flow of AngularJS-based single web applications, providing a novel test criterion. Authors present a running example which is the core of the case study described. Finally, authors plan to extend the analysis by more AngularJS directives such as *ng-repeat* and *$watch*.

The second paper written by In-Young Ko, KyeongDeok Baek, Jung-Hyun Kwon, Hernan Lira, and HyeongCehol Moon, present a framework to test and verify the reliability and safety of cyber physical system (CPS) applications in the perspectives of cyber physical system environments and users. This framework includes a metric and an algorithm for testing and choosing the most effective services that can deliver effects from their associated physical devices to users. In addition, it provides a computational model to test whether a CPS application may cause a cognitive depletion or contention problems for users.

For further information and material, such as the slides of the presentations, please visit the website of MATWEP 2019: http://www.iwt2.org/matwep2019/.

Acknowledgement

We like to express our gratitude to the authors and presenters for the well-prepared presentations, all the workshop participants for their questions and comments, the MATWEP Program Committee that did a great job reviewing the submitted papers, and the ICWE 2019 Organizing Committee for their excellent support. The workshop organizers have been supported by the Pololas project (TIN2016-76956-C3-2-R) of the Spanish Ministry of Economy and Competitiveness.

Organization

Program Committee

Piero Fraternali	Politecnico di Milano, Italy
Gustavo Rossi	LIFIA-F. Informatica, UNLP, Argentina
Carlos Torrecilla-Salinas	IWT2 Group, Spain
Marco Winckler	Université Nice Sophia Antipolis (Polytecj), France
David Lizcano	Madrid Open University, UDIMA
Piero Fraternali	Politecnico di Milano
María José Escalona	University of Seville
Margaret Ross	Solent University of Southampton

Scenario Testing of AngularJS-Based Single Page Web Applications

Gefei Zhang[1]($\boxtimes$) and Jianjun Zhao[2]

[1] Hochschule für Technik und Wirtschaft Berlin, Berlin, Germany
`gefei.zhang@htw-berlin.de`
[2] Kyushu University, Fukuoka, Japan
`zhao@ait.kyushu-u.ac.jp`

Abstract. AngularJS is a popular framework for single page web applications. Due to separation of programming logic and GUI, the data and control flow in AngularJS applications are usually hard to track. We propose a white-box method for first integrating the separate concerns into one interaction diagram, which contains the overall data and control flow of a program, and then separating user interactions from each other. With the help of the interactions, our method helps to achieve a better understanding of AgnularJS-based single page web applications, and moreover provides novel test coverage criteria for them.

1 Introduction

AngularJS [3] is one of the modern frontend-frameworks which support the Model-View-ViewModel architecture (MVVM) [13]: the models provide data to the application, the views define the graphical presentation of the data, and the view-models (also called controllers) define the business logic (data and control flows) of the application. Usually, views are defined in HTML, models and controllers in Javascript.

AngularJS is widely used in single page web applications (SPA). In an SPA, the application has only one HTML page, containing an array of widgets. When the user gives some input in one widget, the application reacts and updates some other widgets. Between the widgets of the page there may or may not exist data and control flow, and a widget may or may not be influenced by another one. Since data and control flow is defined in the controller, separately from the widgets, potential interactions may be obscure; generation of test cases and definition of test coverage criteria may be hard.

We present a method to analyse AngularJS-based SPA. We create an *Interaction Diagram* by translating HTML widgets, as well as functions and variables in the controller to nodes, and the invocation, reading and writing relationships between them as edges. The interaction diagram not only visualizes possible

Partially supported by the EU project cAPITs and the German BMBF project deep. TEACHING (01IS17056).

M. Brambilla et al. (Eds.): ICWE 2019 Workshops, LNCS 11609, pp. 91–103, 2020.
https://doi.org/10.1007/978-3-030-51253-8_10

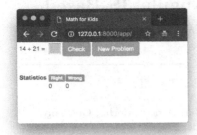 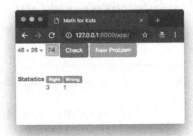

(a) The system waiting for the user to en- (b) The system gives a verdict and updates
ter an answer   statistics

Fig. 1. Example: math exercises with statistics

workflows of the application, but also allows us to define user-action centered
test coverage criteria. In this paper, we show how to isolate the widgets that are
involved in an interaction from those that are not, and how to use this knowledge
to define test coverage criteria.

The rest of this paper is organized as follows: In the following Sect. 2, we give a
brief introduction to AngularJS, and also present our running example. Section 3
introduces interaction diagrams. In Sect. 4 we show how to analyse workflows of
the application and define test coverage criteria using the interaction diagram.
Related work is discussed in Sect. 5. Finally, in Sect. 6, we conclude and outline
some future work.

2   AngularJS

We first give a brief introduction to AngularJS by means of a simple example,
and then define an abstract syntax for AngularJS applications. Due to space
limitation, we focus on a small subset of AngularJS; it is relatively straightforward to extend our approach to cover other features of the framework.

2.1   Running Example

Figure 1 shows an AngularJS application to teach kids addition. In the upper
part an addition problem is presented, the lower part shows statistics of how
many right and wrong answers the user has given. When a new problem is
shown, the user can enter her answer in an input field (Fig. 1(a)), the system
then shows if the answer is right or wrong. Meanwhile, a new button appears.
When the user clicks on it, a new problem is generated (Fig. 1(b)). In the lower
part of the browser, a statistics is shown of how many right and wrong answers
the user has given. In Fig. 1(b), the user has answered four questions in total,
where three of the answers were correct, and one was wrong.

2.2 Data Binding

In AngularJS, the program logic is implemented in a so-called *controller* in Javascript, and the graphical layout of the application is defined in a *template* in the HTML syntax, with some special attributes of HTML tags, which are defined by AngularJS and called *directives*. The template of the running example is shown in Fig. 2,[1] where we removed styles of the HTML elements from the listing for simplicity. The controller is written in Javascript, and provides data and event handlers for the application. The controller of the running example is listed in Fig. 3.

The communication between template and controller takes place in the controller's variable $scope. Just like every other object in Javascript (cf. [8]), $scope is also a collection of key-value pairs. In Javascript, the keys are called *properties*. The value of a key can be any object, and in particular, any function. For example, in lines 4 and 5, Fig. 3, $scope is extended by two properties count_right and count_wrong with initial value 0. In lines 17, the property may_check is assigned a function. In Javascript, function properties are usually not changed after initial assignment, while other properties are often overwritten and used as variables. We therefore call the latter *variable properties*.

The Javascript object $scope is the controller's interface to the template: its properties (e.g., $scope.count_right in line 4 and $scope.check_answer defined in lines 21 to 25) are visible to the template, and may be bound to HTML elements to provide data or event handlers. Other top-level functions and variables of the controller (e.g., c in line 7 and add_problem defined in lines 8 to 15), which are not properties of $scope, are only for "private" use in the controller and not visible to the template.

Data flow between template and controller is defined by *data binding*: an HTML element in the template may be *bound* to a property of the object $scope of the controller, and gets updated automatically when the value of the property changes. Data binding is defined in so-called directives; directives are included in the template as attributes of HTML elements.

AngularJS supports both *one-way* and *two-way* data binding. The directive ng-bind or double braces {{}} define one-way data binding, that is, the HTML element automatically presents the up-to-date value of the bound property of $scope, whilst changes of the value presented by the HTML element, if any, would not be propagated from the GUI back to the from the controller (the $scope).[2] For instance, in Fig. 2, line 5, {{a}} and {{b}} will be replaced by the values of the variables $scope.a and $scope.b at runtime, respectively. The values of the two variables are assigned in function add_problem of the controller (Fig. 3, lines 11 and 12). A little more examination of the controller reveals that this function is called to generate a new addition problem, and $scope.a and $scope.b hold the values of the two summands.

---

[1] The project is available under https://bitbucket.org/gefei/angularjs-example.

[2] There is some subtle difference between the semantics of ng-bind and double braces, see https://stackoverflow.com/a/16126174. However, the difference is not relevant for our discussion. In this paper, we consider ng-bind and double braces as equivalent.

```
1   <html>
2   <body ng-app="app">
3   <div ng-controller="controller">
4     <form>
5     {{a}} + {{b}} = <input ng-model="answer">
6     <button ng-disabled="!may_check()"
7        ng-click="input_answer()">Check</button>
8     <button ng-if="right===true">Right</button>
9     <button ng-if="right===false">Wrong</button>
10    <button ng-click="new_problem()">New Problem</button>
11    </form>
12    <hr>
13
14    <table>
15      <tr>
16        <th>Statistics</td>
17        <th><span>Right</span></td>
18        <th><span>Wrong</span></td>
19      </tr>
20      <tr>
21      <td></td>
22      <td><span ng-bind="count_right"></span></td>
23      <td><span ng-bind="count_wrong"></span></td>
24      </tr>
25    </table>
26  </div>
27  </body>
28  </html>
```

Fig. 2. HTML template

Other directives defining one-way data binding include ng-if and ng-disabled. In ng-if, the value of the bound property is not shown; instead it regulates the visibility of the HTML element: if and only if the Javascript expression bound to ng-if is valued to true is the HTML element visible in the GUI. For example, both of the two buttons defined in lines 8 and 9 of Fig. 2 are guarded with ng-if. The conditions for the buttons being visible are the variable $scope.right being true and false, respectively. Figure 3 shows that the variable is set in line 22, in function $scope.input_answer, and is true iff the value of variable c equals to the value of $scope.answer parsed as an integer.

Directive ng-disabled is used to set HTML widgets disabled (i.e., the user cannot enter her input). In line 6 of Fig. 2, the button is disabled when the negation of the result of function $scope.may_check(), which is defined in the lines 17–19 of Fig. 3. The function returns true iff the input field is not empty (!!$scope.answer) and $scope.right is still undefined (i.e., the button Check has not been clicked yet, see Sect. 2.3). When this is the case, the function returns true, ng-disabled receives the value false, then the button is disabled, and vice versa.

```
 1   var app = angular.module('app', []);
 2
 3   app.controller('controller', function($scope){
 4       $scope.count_right = 0;
 5       $scope.count_wrong = 0;
 6
 7       var c;
 8       function add_problem() {
 9           var max = 100;
10           c = Math.floor(Math.random() * (max - 1)) + 1;
11           $scope.a = Math.floor(Math.random() * (c - 2)) + 1;
12           $scope.b = c - $scope.a;
13           $scope.answer = undefined;
14           $scope.right = undefined;
15       }
16
17       $scope.may_check = function() {
18           return !!$scope.answer && $scope.right === undefined;
19       }
20
21       $scope.check_answer = function() {
22           $scope.right = c === parseInt($scope.answer);
23           $scope.count_right += ($scope.right) ? 1 : 0;
24           $scope.count_wrong += ($scope.right) ? 0 : 1;
25       };
26
27       $scope.new_problem = function() {
28           add_problem();
29       }
30
31       add_problem();
32   })
```

Fig. 3. Controller

We call the property of $scope that an HTML element is bound to the *target* of the data binding, and the HTML element the *source*. While ng-bind and {{}} show the value of the target in the GUI, ng-if and ng-disabled do not output the value in the textual form. It rather *influences* the appearance of the source by setting its visibility or enabled/disabled status. In both cases, we say the source of a data binding *presents* the value of the target.

The directive ng-model defines *two-way* data binding, that is, the widget automatically updates when the value of its bound property changes, and any change of the widget's value will be propagated to the bound variable. Therefore, a bidirectional data flow is defined. For instance, in line 5 of Fig. 2, the input element has an attribute ng-model=answer. The input field is therefore bound to the variable $scope.answer: the value of the input field is hold in $scope.answer, changes are propagated automatically in both directions. In Fig. 3, the correct answer of the current problem is stored in variable c (line 10), and $scope.right is calculated by a comparison with $scope.answer in line 22.

The target of a one-way data binding may be a variable property or a function property of $scope. If it is a variable property, the source presents the target's value. If it is a function property, the widget presents the return value of the function. On the other hand, the target of a two-way data binding must be a variable property, since the target must store the value of the user input, and only a variable, as opposed to a function, can be assigned a value.

The template of the statistics is defined in an HTML table (lines 14 to 25 in Fig. 2), where two td cells (lines 22 and 23) present the values of $scope.count_right and $scope.count_wrong by one-way data binding.

2.3   Event Handling

HTML elements may also be provided with event handlers. Upon the given event, the specified function is executed. For example, in line 7 of Fig. 2, the directive ng-click binds the function $scope.input_answer to the button. Therefore, the function is invoked when the user clicks the button. The function is defined in Fig. 3, lines 21 to 25. When invoked, it first (line 22) checks if c has the same value as $scope.answer (which we know is the current value of the user input in the text field, see Sect. 2.2), parsed as an integer, and assigns the result to $scope.right. Then, depending on if $scope.right is true or not, the value $scope.count_right or $scope.count_wrong is incremented by one. Therefore, the statistics gets updated when the user clicks the Check button (Fig. 2, lines 22 and 23).

The button New Problem also has an event handler: in Fig. 2, line 10, the directive ng-click="new_problem()" binds the function $scope.new_problem to handle the event of the button being clicked. The function calls another function add_problem to generate a new problem by updating the values of $scope.a, $scope.b, setting c, to be undefined to clear the field for the user to input her answer (recall: this field has a two-way data binding, as defined in line 5 of Fig. 2), setting both $scope.right and $scope.answer to be undefined. Therefore, when New Problem is clicked, $scope.may_check will return true, and the button Check will get enabled (Fig. 2, line 6).

Variable c and function new_problem are not defined as $scope's properties. Therefore, they are local to the controller, and not exposed to the template.

2.4   Abstract Syntax

An AngularJS-based SPA is a tuple (T, C, D, E). T is a template, written in HTML and consisting of a set of HTML tags $(T = \{h\})$ which define HTML widgets,[3] C is the definition of a controller, written in Javascript, D is a set of data bindings, and E is a set of event handler bindings.

---

[3] Precisely, HTML tags may be nested, thus the HTML template is a tree. In this paper, we do not consider nesting tags, and just view the template as a set.

The controller definition C is modeled as a tuple $(V, F, \$scope)$, where V is a set of top-level variables, F is a set of top-level functions, and $\$scope \in V$ is a distinguished element of V. We write $V(\$scope)$ for the set of $\$scope$'s variable properties, and $F(\$scope)$ for the set of $\$scope$'s function properties. We define $W = V\backslash\{\$scope\}$ to be the set of top-level variables defined in the controller other than $\$scope$. We also define function $init \in F$ to be a distinguished function which does the necessary initialisation of the controller. Without loss of generality we assume that such an $init$ exists in each AngularJS application (in our example, it is the function add_problem, invoked in line 31 in Fig. 3). If in an application no such initial function is defined explicitly, then we assume $init$ sets default values to the widgets.

D is the set of data binding relations between HTML tags and variable properties of $\$scope$: $D \subseteq \{(h, V(\$scope) \cup F(\$scope)\}$. Given $d = (n, o) \in D$, we define $source(d) = n$ and $target(d) = o$. Two-way data bindings build a subset $D' \subseteq D$, and $\forall d \in D'$, it holds that $target(d) \in V(\$scope)$.

E is the set of event handler bindings between HTML tags and function properties of $\$scope$: $E \subset \{(h, F(\$scope))\}$.

Additionally, for each $f \in F \cup F(\$scope)$, we define $R(f) \subseteq V \cup V(\$scope)$ and $W(f) \subseteq V \cup V(\$scope)$ to be the set of the variables f reads from and writes to, respectively. We also define $Inv(f) \subset F$ to be the functions invoked by f.[4] In this paper, we take these sets for granted. Since Javascript is an "extremely dynamic" [11] language, this is in general not always the case. However, in modern software development, *readability first* is considered best practice, and it is reasonable to assume that at least reading, writing, and invocation relationships can be obtained by simple analysis.

3   Interaction Diagram

In order to understand the workflow of the application, it is necessary to study both its HTML and its Javascript code, as well as their interactions. We now present Interaction Diagrams to visualize the overall behavior, combining the logic defined in HTML and Javascript. Figure 4 shows the interaction diagram for our running example.

An Interaction Diagram ID is a directed graph (N, E). The set of nodes is defined as the union of three sets: $N = N_H \cup N_{\$scope} \cup N_{js}$, where, using the notations introduced in Sect. 2.4,

- for each $(h, v) \in D$, we generate a node n_h, and $N_H = \{n_h \mid (h, v) \in D\}$. Graphically, we label n_h with the label of h, or, if h does not have a label, the name of the target of the data binding (without $\$scope$), extended by the position of the definition of h in the template;
- for each $(h, v) \in D$, we create a node n_v, and for each $(h, e) \in E$, we create a node n_e. $N_{\$scope}$ is then defined as $N_{\$scope} = \{n_v \mid (h, v) \in D\} \cup \{n_e \mid (h, e) \in$

---

[4] Although it is also possible for a $\$scope$ function to call another $\$scope$ function, it is usually not necessary and not a good idea.

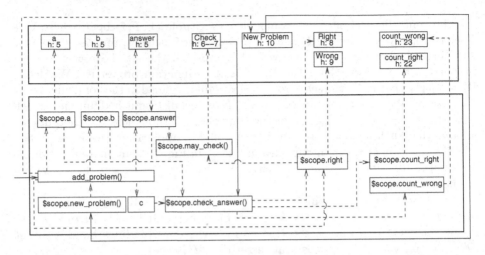

Fig. 4. Interaction diagram

E}. Graphically, we label each $n_f \in N_{\$scope}$ with the name of the f (with $scope), but do not include the position of f's appearances in the controller.
– for each $v \in W$, we create a node n_v; for each $f \in F$, we create a node n_f, and $N_{js} = \{n_v \mid v \in W\} \cup \{n_f \mid f \in F\}$. Graphically, we label these nodes with the name of the variable or function. Additionally, for the initial function *init*, we distinguish n_{init} by an arrow without starting vertex and pointing to n_{init}.

For example, Fig. 4 shows the interaction diagram for our running example. The upper compartment shows N_H, which contains a node for each of the text fields a, b (which show the two summands to the user), $scope.answer (where the user may enter her answer), the buttons Check (which the user may click to check if the answer is correct), the labels Right and Wrong (which show the result of the check to the user), the labels count_right and count_wrong (which show the current success statistics of the user), and the button New Problem (which the user may click to generate a new problem).

The lower compartment models components of the controller. It contains the elements of $N_{\$scope}$ and N_{js}. That is, it contains a node for each of the variables $scope.a, $scope.b (which hold the values of the summands), $scope.answer (which holds the answer inputted by the user), $scope.right (which holds the value $scope.check_answer returns, see below), $scope.count_right and $scope.count_wrong (which hold the current number of right and wrong answers the user has given), and the functions $scope.check_answer (which checks if the answer inputted by the user is correct), and $scope.new_problem (which generates the summands and key of a new problem). The lower compartment also contains a node for c, which holds the key of the new problem. Moreover, for scope.add_problem() is marked as the initial function.

The edges E of the interaction diagram are used to model data and control flow. We define E as the union of seven subsets: $E = E_{data} \cup E'_{data} \cup E_{event} \cup E_W \cup E_R \cup E_{Inv} \cup E_{init}$, where

- for each $d \in D$, we create an edge $e_d = (\text{target}(d), \text{source}(d))$. The set of all data-flow edges from the controller to HTML widgets is then modeled as $E_{data} = \{e_d \mid d \in D\}$. If $d \in D'$, we additionally create an edge $e'_t = (\text{source}(t), \text{target}(t))$ to model the HTML widget reading value from its bound variable. The set of all data-flow edges from HTML widgets to the controller is then modeled as $E'_{data} = \{e_d \mid d \in D'\}$,
- for each $(h, f) \in E$, we define an event-handling edge $e_h = (n_h, n_f)$. The set of all event-handling relation is then modeled as $E_{event} = \{e_h \mid (h, f) \in E\}$,
- for each pair (f, v), $f \in F \cup F(\$scope)$, $v \in W(f)$, we create an edge $e_{f,v}$. The set of writing relations is then modeled as $E_W = \bigcup_{f \in F \cup F(\$scope)} \{e_{f,v} \mid v \in W(f)\}$. For each pair (v, f), $f \in F \cup F(\$scope)$, $v \in R(f)$, we create an edge $e_{v,f}$. The set of reading relations is then modeled as $E_R = \bigcup_{f \in F \cup F(\$scope)} \{e_{v,f} \mid v \in R(f)\}$,
- for each $f \in F \cup F(\$scope)$ and each $v \in \text{Inv}(f)$, we create an edge $e_{f,v}$. The relations of a function writing a variable is then modeled by $E_{Inv} = \bigcup_{f \in F \cup F(\$scope)} \{e_{v,f} \mid v \in \text{Inv}(f)\}$,
- for each $h \in H$, where $\nexists v$ such that $(h, v) \in D$, we create an edge $e_{init,h}$. The set of all edges of (fictive) setting default values of widgets is then modeled by $E_{init} = \bigcup_{h \in T, \forall v, (h,v) \notin D} \{e_{init,h}\}$.

Graphically, we use a dashed-line arrow to represent each $e \in E_{data} \cup E'_{data} \cup E_W \cup E_R \cup E_{Inv} \cup E_{init}$, and a solid-line arrow to represent each $e \in E_{event}$. Note for event handling, the exact event is not modeled, and it does not need to be modeled in an Interaction Diagram.

In our example (see Fig. 4), the elements of E_{data} model one-way data binding: ($scope.a, a), ($scope.b, b), ($scope.count_right, count_right), ($scope.count_wrong, count_wrong), ($scope.right, Right), ($scope.wrong, Wrong), and ($scope.may_check(), Check). E'_{data} contains the two edges between $scope.answer and answer, modeling the only two-way data binding in the example. E_{event} contains the two edges (Check, $scope.check_answer()) and (New Problem, $scope.new_problem()).

Furthermore, E_W contains the four edges leaving add_problem(), and the edges leaving $scope.check_answer(). E_R contains the edges from c to $scope.check_answer(), and from $scope.answer to $scope.may_check(). E_{Inv} contains the edge from $scope.new_problem() to add_problem(). Finally, E_{init} contains the edge from add_problem() to New Problem.

4 Testing

SPAs are interactive: the user makes some input, the system reacts and makes updates to some widgets, then the user makes another input, and so on. We define an interaction to be a round of user giving input, and the system updating widgets accordingly. It is desirable to define interaction-based tests. An interaction can be triggered explicitly by the user invoking an event handler, or implicitly while the user is updating data, which is bound by ng-model.

4.1 Interactions

Starting from interaction diagrams, it is easy to "slice" interactions, i.e, to find out the widgets that get updated upon a certain piece of user input or is set up by the initial function.

A widget t reacts to another widget s iff in the interaction diagram t's representation n_t is reachable from s's presentation n_s, and the only event-handling edge, if any, on the path from n_s to n_t event-handling edge is the very first edge (leaving n_s) on the path. This edge models the interaction being explicitly triggered.

Formally, given a node $n \in N_H \cup \{init\}$, we say a node $m \in N_H$ *reacts to* n iff

1. $\exists n_0, n_1, n_2, \ldots n_k \in N, n_0 = n, n_k = m$ such that for each $0 \le i < k$, $(n_i, n_{i+1}) \in E$, and
2. $\forall n_p, 1 < p \le k$ and $\forall e \in E, \mathsf{target}(e) = n_p$ it holds that $e \notin E_{event}$.

We write $I(n)$ for the set of all nodes representing the widgets that react to n. This set contains the widgets that are automatically updated upon user input, and thus constitute an interaction. To analyze interactions in the SPA, we calculate for each *input widget*, i.e., widget with an edge leaving it in the interaction diagram. Based on Fig. 4, we can calculate the following three interactions for our running example:

- $I(\text{add\_problem}()) = \{a, b, \text{answer}\}$, which means when the application starts, the value of these three fields are set automatically,
- $I(\text{answer}) = \{\text{Check}, \text{answer}\}$, which means when the user is entering her answer, answer (which is trivial) and Check (enabled) are updated. Note that updating the answer does not trigger $\text{scope.check\_answer}()$, since this function needs explicit triggering viaCheck,
- $I(\text{Check}) = \{\text{Check}, \text{Right}, \text{Wrong}, \text{count\_right}, \text{count\_wrong}\}$, which means when the user clicks on Check, these widgets get an update: the button itself (disabled), one of Right and Wrong is displayed, indicating whether the user-inputted answer is correct, and one of the counts also gets updated.
- $I(\text{New Problem}) = \{a, b, \text{answer}, \text{Check}, \text{Right}, \text{Wrong}\}$, which means when the user clicks New Problem, the widgets a, b (showing the summands of the new problem), answer (emptied), Check (enabled), as well as Right and Wrong (both made invisible), are updated.

The interactions define an upper bound of what *might* get modified when the user makes input in other widgets. For instance, according to the analysis, when the user clicks the button Check, then all the labels Right, Wrong, count_right, count_wrong might get modified, although only one of Right and Wrong, and only one of count_right and count_wrong will actually be modified. However, this upper bound gives us a good starting point to define test coverage criteria.

4.2 Coverage Criteria

The interactions should not be tested in isolation. For reasonable tests, we need some interactions to set up the stage for others. For instance, in our running example, testing the implementation of the event handler of the button Check is only possible after the user has inputted a value in the field answer.

In the following, we use the notation defined above that an AngularJS SPA is a tuple $S = (T, C, D, E)$, where T is the set of all HTML elements in the template, and $init$ is the initial function. We also define the set $\mathcal{I} = \{w \in T \mid I(w) \neq \emptyset\}$.

Interactions can be triggered automatically by the initial function, or by the user actions like changing the value of an input field or clicking with the mouse. We refer to a sequence of user actions as a *scenario*. For convenience, we also call the initial function a user action. Actually this function is invoked by the user launching the application. For any scenario $A = (a_0, a_1, \ldots, a_n)$, we require $a_0 = init$, and $\forall 0 < k \leq n, a_k \in \mathcal{I}$. Given $A = (a_0, a_1, \ldots, a_n)$, we define $I(A) = I(a_n)$. Moreover, given $x \in \mathcal{I}$, we also define $A \oplus x = (a_0, a_1, \ldots, a_n, x)$.

We define the initial set of test scenarios $\mathcal{S}_0 = \{(init)\}$. The only scenario contained in this set is the initial function. It is invoked automatically when the application is started. No user input is involved.

For $n > 0$, $\mathcal{S}_{n+1} = \{p \oplus x \mid p \in \mathcal{S}_n, x \in I(p) \cap \mathcal{I}\}$. That is, we prolong each scenario contained in sce_n by every widget where the user can take an action. We repeat this until all $i \in \mathcal{I}$ is included in some scenario.

Applied to our example, we get three sets of test scenarios:

- $\mathcal{S}_0 = \{\text{add\_problem()}\}$
- $\mathcal{S}_1 = \{(\text{add\_problem()}, \text{answer}), (\text{add\_problem()}, \text{New Problem})\}$
- $\mathcal{S}_2 = \{(\text{add\_problem()}, \text{answer}, \text{Check}), (\text{add\_problem()}, \text{New Problem}, \text{Check})\}$

Based on the sets of test scenarios, it is easy to define our coverage criteria:

- Each set $\mathcal{S}_n$ of test scenarios should be tested.
- For each given $\mathcal{S}_n$, each $p \in \mathcal{S}_n$ should be tested.
- For each given p, each $w \in I(p)$ should be tested. That is, there should be a test case for each widget that may be modified after the scenario p.

Applied to our example, we get

- Considering $\mathcal{S}_0$, since $I(\text{add\_problem()}) = \{a, b, \text{answer}\}$, there should be test cases checking the status of a, b, answer after the application initialisation.
- Considering $\mathcal{S}_1$, since $I(\text{anwer}) = \{\text{Check}, \text{answer}\}$, there should be test cases checking the status of Check and answer after the application has been initialized and the user makes input in the field answer. Moreover, since $I(\text{New Problem}) = \{a, b, \text{answer}, \text{Check}, \text{Right}, \text{Wrong}\}$, there should be test cases checking the status of these six widgets after the application has been initialized and the user clicks the button New Problem.
- Analog for $\mathcal{S}_2$.

5   Related Work

Analysis of Javascript programs, in particular their test coverage criteria, is a very dynamic research field, see e.g. [2,6,7]. Due to the very dynamic nature of the language, its analysis is not an easy task, see [11] for an overview. One of the challenges is the interactions between browser, DOM and Javascript. In [4,10], a unified API is given to formalise the browser behavior. However, large-scale libraries are still difficult to analyze, and therefore their functionalities are often modeled manually. Our work is also along this line in that we also take the semantics of AngularJS for granted.

For the analysis of such frameworks, it is essential to understand their interactions [11]. This is exactly where our work is positioned. Other interesting publications in this area include [9], which provides a method of checking name and type consistency between template and controller, and [1], where the authors present a hybrid method for change impact analysis, and its focused on plain Javascript, without frameworks. Compared with these approaches, our focus is on the analysis of boundaries of interactions and defining a set of test criteria for applications based on a complex framework.

An approach to teaching AngularJS applications is provided in [12], which uses state machines to do black-box testing. In comparison, our proposal is a white-box approach.

6   Conclusions and Future Work

We presented a method for analysing AngularJS-based single page web applications. Based on the interaction diagrams, our approach provides an easy means to understand the control and data flow of AngulaJS-base SPA, and to define a novel test criteria.

We are currently working on an extension of our tool [5] for interaction analysis to cover test case generation as well. In the future, we plan to extend the analysis by more AngularJS directives such as ng-repeat and $watch.

References

1. Alimadadi, S., Mesbah, A., Pattabiraman, K.: Hybrid DOM-sensitive change impact analysis for JavaScript. In: Proceedings of the 29th European Conference on Object-Oriented Programming (ECOOP 2015), pp. 321–345 (2015)
2. Dhok, M., Ramanathan, M.K., Sinha, N.: Type-aware concolic testing of JavaScript programs, pp. 168–179. ACM (2016)
3. Google. AngularJS. https://angularjs.org/
4. Jensen, S.H., Madsen, M., Møller, A.: Modeling the HTML DOM and browser API in static analysis of JavaScript Web Applications. In: Proceedings of the 19th ACM SIGSOFT Symposium Foundations of Software Engineering and 13th European Software Engineering Conference (FSE/ESEC 2011), pp. 59–69. ACM (2011)
5. Materne, D.: Interaktionsanalayse von AngularJS-Programmen. Master's thesis, Hochschule für Technik und Wirtschaft Berlin (2018). (in German)

6. Mesbah, A.: Advances in testing JavaScript-based Web Applications. Adv. Comput. **97**, 201–235 (2015)
7. Mirshokraie, S., Mesbah, A., Pattabiraman, K.: JSEFT: automated Javascript unit test generation. In: 8th IEEE International Conference on Software Testing, Verification and Validation, ICST 2015, pp. 1–10. IEEE Computer Society (2015)
8. Mozilla. JavaScript object basics (2018). https://developer.mozilla.org/en-US/docs/Learn/JavaScript/Objects/Basics
9. Ocariza Jr., F.S., Pattabiraman, K., Mesbah, A.: Detecting inconsistencies in JavaScript MVC applications. In: Proceedings of the 37th International Conference on Software Engineering (ICSE 2015), vol. 1, pp. 325–335. IEEE Computer Society (2015)
10. Park, C., Won, S., Jin, J., Ryu, S.: Static analysis of JavaScript Web Applications in the wild via practical DOM modeling. In: Proceedings of the 30th International Conference on Automated Software Engineering (ASE 2015), pp. 552–562. IEEE Computer Society (2015)
11. Sun, K., Ryu, S.: Analysis of JavaScript programs: challenges and research trends. ACM Comput. Surv. **50**(4), 59:1–59:34 (2017)
12. van Deursen, A.: Testing Web Applications with state objects. Comm. ACM **58**(8), 36–43 (2015)
13. Wikipedia. Model view ViewModel (2015). https://en.wikipedia.org/w/index.php?title=Model_View_ViewModel&oldid=675433955

Environment-Aware and Human-Centric Software Testing Framework for Cyber-Physical Systems

In-Young Ko[(✉)], KyeongDeok Baek[(✉)], Jung-Hyun Kwon, Hernan Lira, and HyeongCehol Moon

School of Computing, Korea Advanced Institute of Science and Technology, Daejeon, Republic of Korea
{iko,kyeongdeok.baek,junghyun.kwon,lirahernan,hc.moon}@kaist.ac.kr

Abstract. The functionalities, actuations and effects that are produced by an application of a cyber physical system (CPS) are usually consumed by users while they perform their daily activities. Therefore, it is critical to ensure that they do not interfere with human activities and do not harm the people who are involved in the CPS. In this paper, we propose a framework to test and verify the reliability and safety of CPS applications in the perspectives of CPS environments and users. The framework provides an environment-aware testing method by which the efficiency of testing CPS applications can be improved by prioritizing CPS environments, and by applying machine learning techniques. The framework also includes a metric and an algorithm by which we can test and choose the most effective services that can deliver effects from their associated physical devices to users. In addition, the framework provides a computational model to test whether a CPS application may cause a cognitive depletion or contention problems for users.

Keywords: Environment-aware testing · Service effects · Human cognitive resources · Service-oriented CPS software

1 Introduction

A *cyber-physical system (CPS)* is a system in which computational and physical resources are connected and coordinated to produce functionalities, actuations, and effects that are necessary to accomplish a user's goal [1]. Various types of CPS such as autonomous vehicles, and smart factories have been assimilated into our daily lives. In particular, CPS applications that utilize *Internet of Things (IoT)* resources are becoming more popular among people globally.

This research was supported by the Next-Generation Information Computing Development Program through the National Research Foundation of Korea (NRF) funded by the Ministry of Science, ICT (NRF-2017M3C4A7066210).

M. Brambilla et al. (Eds.): ICWE 2019 Workshops, LNCS 11609, pp. 104–115, 2020.
https://doi.org/10.1007/978-3-030-51253-8_11

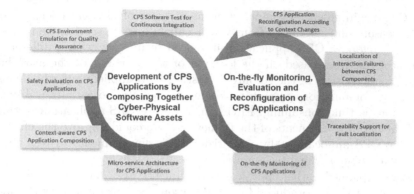

Fig. 1. DevOps for CPS software

One of the essential characteristics of CPS applications is that the functionalities, actuations, and effects that are produced by a CPS application are usually experienced by users while they perform their daily activities. In addition, in some cases, human beings become a part of CPS, providing essential capabilities that are needed to accomplish a goal. Therefore, most CPS applications must be reliable and safe so that they do not interfere with human activities and do not harm those who are involved in a CPS.

Traditional software testing tests applications by verifying code using a set of predefined or automatically generated test cases. These test cases usually produce inputs and events that affect the behavior of the software, and the correct behavior of the software can be verified by checking the outputs that are generated when running test cases. Unlike in traditional software, outputs of a CPS application are affected not only by the behavior of the implemented code but also by the characteristics of the running environment and the circumstances of users. Therefore, to ensure the reliability and safety of CPS, we need a new means of effectively testing CPS applications while considering their running environments, and the conditions and context of users.

In this study, we propose a framework to test and verify the reliability and safety of CPS applications according to CPS environments and the users that closely interact with CPS applications. The testing framework is built atop the service-oriented CPS software architecture that we defined in our previous work [5]. This service-oriented CPS architecture allows developers to build CPS applications by defining and composing services as building blocks. We also consider the DevOps practices to define the process of testing and verifying CPS applications during the developmental and operational phases in an iterative and incremental manner. Figure 1 shows the DevOps activities of composing, testing, monitoring, and reconfiguring CPS applications in our framework. In this study, we focus on testing, on-the-fly monitoring, and dynamic reconfiguration activities in this DevOps process.

A CPS environment is composed of many types of physical resources such as IoT sensors and actuators from which capabilities of services can be produced. Therefore, a CPS application may need to interact with a different set of physical resources based on the location of the user and/or the availability of QoS characteristics of the resources. Testing CPS applications while considering many combinations of physical resources that are potentially utilized for applications is time-consuming. Environment-aware CPS-application testing is one of the major components of the framework. We could improve the efficiency of testing CPS applications by prioritizing CPS environments to test and by applying machine learning techniques.

As we explained earlier, physical environments also affect the delivery of service effects that are produced from CPS resources. Our framework includes a metric and an algorithm used to test and choose the most effective services that can deliver visual effects from their associated IoT resources to users. In addition, the framework provides a computational model to assess the types and number of user cognitive resources that are necessary to use a set of services from a CPS application along with everyday human activities. By using the model, we can test whether a CPS application may cause a cognitive depletion or contention problems, which might lead the user to an unstable or dangerous situation.

In Sect. 2, we describe the service-oriented CPS framework. We explain the core elements of the environment-aware and human-centric CPS software testing framework in Sect. 3. The preliminary results derived from the approaches we developed for the testing framework are shown and discussed in Sect. 4. We explain related works in Sect. 5, and conclude the paper in Sect. 6.

2   Service-Oriented CPS Application Framework

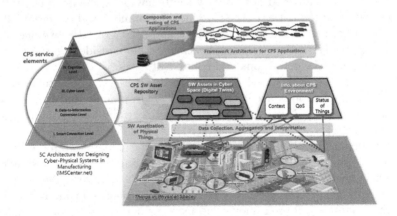

Fig. 2. Service-oriented CPS application framework based on 5C CPS architecture

Existing software engineering efforts related to CPS focus primarily on developing CPS platforms or domain-specific applications. In addition, most CPS platforms and applications have been developed based on different development principles and by using different methods and tools. Unlike traditional software environments, CPS is regarded as a system of systems that are associated with diverse and heterogeneous cyber and physical systems and operates in a variety of situations that can be difficult to predict.

The left side of Fig. 2 shows the 5C architecture for designing CPS systems, which is composed of connection, conversion, cyber, cognition, and configuration layers [8]. The connection layer is composed of various types of physical things (sensors and actuators) that are connected to network environments. At the conversion layer, the data obtained from the physical things are aggregated and converted into useful information that can be used to mine valuable patterns and to predict future trends and potential problems. This is done by maintaining and analyzing virtual representations (digital twins) of physical things at the cyber layer. The crucial patterns, trends, and problems can be visualized for human consumption at the cognition layer, and the system can be reconfigured to improve its capabilities and solve problems based on human decisions at the configuration layer. The CPS elements in the 5C architecture are usually heterogeneous in terms of their interfaces and functional/data semantics, and their availability and functional/data quality may be changed dynamically over time. To address these problems effectively, we have developed a service-oriented CPS application framework based on the 5C CPS architecture.

In this framework, all physical and computational elements in the 5C architecture are servicized to make them accessible through standard service interfaces. Figure 2 shows the servicization process for the CPS elements. This enables the heterogeneous CPS elements to inter-operate effectively for an application. Usually, a service is modeled and defined from the user perspective and in terms of achieving a task goal of a user. In other words, the capabilities of CPS services are represented by using common semantics that are closely related to user activities for achieving a task goal in a specific application domain. Each service provides its service capabilities by utilizing one or more physical devices. This helps application developers to choose effectively and integrate relevant CPS services for a user task while overcoming the semantic heterogeneity of service functions and data. In addition, this CPS application framework provides the basis for ensuring the reliability and safety of CPS applications.

As shown in the right side of Fig. 2, a CPS environment is composed of various devices that are scattered in a physical space. Therefore, considering the characteristics of physical environments and users is essential for generating and delivering high-quality service effects to users. In particular, the context or perception of a user in a CPS environment as well as the status or QoS of physical devices are critical to enable the user to consume the service effects through the physical environment. We have developed a service description model and a selection method to choose the services the effects from which can be consumed by users in an effective manner. The next section provides more details on this environment-aware service selection method.

3 Environment-Aware and Human-Centric CPS Software Testing

The runtime environments of a CPS application can vary depending on the combinations of available elements in physical and cyber spaces. In addition, because the cognitive abilities of users of a CPS application are diverse, considering the cognitive characteristics of users in order to choose and integrate CPS services for a user task is necessary. Therefore, to ensure the reliability and safety of a CPS application, testing the CPS application not only by validating its functionalities but also by identifying defects when running it in various CPS environments and under different user cognition is required.

3.1 Environment-Aware Regression Testing for CPS Applications

Although testing a CPS application in a variety of environments is critical, a CPS application requires more efforts to test than does traditional software. This is because CPS software interacts with physical devices, which can lead to their abnormal operation and can cause not only monetary loss but also inconvenience to CPS software users and even personal injury. Moreover, because a CPS application is operated by using a combination of multiple CPS services, the failure of a CPS application can occur because of defects in both a CPS service and in the CPS application itself. In addition, in various CPS environments, CPS services can behave differently than as indicated by specified requirements, which can lead to more defects. In a DevOps environment where tests are frequently performed, the longer the duration of the tests, the longer the time required for information about environment-related defects to be delivered to the developer. This results in delays in fixing defects and in the release of new versions.

One manner in which to deal with the aforementioned problems is to perform regular regression tests. These tests should be cost-effective in a DevOps environment. Existing cost-effective regression testing techniques may not be appropriate for a DevOps environment because the time between regression tests is shorter in a DevOps environment. In addition, existing techniques require code analysis for each test case, such as code instrumentation and code coverage, which can consume considerable time. Thus, the preparation time for applying existing techniques may be longer than when conducting regression tests in a DevOps environment.

For cost-effective regression testing for CPS applications, we can use test prioritization techniques. Test prioritization techniques involve prioritizing test cases, test suites, or test environments. In a DevOps environment in which regular integration practices are employed, prioritizing test cases or test suites may not be very cost-effective. Therefore, we adopt test environment prioritization techniques for testing CPS applications [7]. Test environment prioritization techniques utilize test history data. In the aforementioned study, we suggested the following five prioritization techniques: exact-matching-based, similarity-matching-based, failure-frequency-based, machine-learning-based, and hybrid. Please refer to the previous study for a description of each technique. Table 1 lists the name of each technique and its code. The codes are used in Sect. 4.1.

Table 1. Technique and its code

Technique	Code	Technique	Code
No ordering	B1	Failure frequency-based	P3
Random ordering	B2	Machine learning-based	P4
Exact match-based	P1	P1 and P3	H1
Similar match-based	P2	P1 and P4	H2

3.2 Effect-Driven Selection of CPS Services

In a CPS environment, a CPS service may produce physical effects such as light or sound via physical devices. Therefore, when evaluating the QoS of a CPS service, considering the quality of the perceived effects of the service according to both the user and traditional quality attributes is necessary.

In our previous study, we proposed a new metric called *spatio-cohesiveness* that measures the manner in which cooperating physical devices of CPS services are located cohesively in a physical space [3]. The rationale behind this concept is that physical effects from services of an application can be successfully consumed by a user only if the cooperating physical devices and the user are in physical proximity. We defined a set of *spatio-cohesiveness requirements*, $r = (m, n, l) \in \mathbf{R}$, that a set of cooperating services must meet. r represents the distance between two services or a service and a user, m, and n, and it should be less than constraint l. The degree to which a requirement is met, $r(\mathbf{S})$, is defined as the normalized distance between two services or a service and a user according to the maximum distance specified, which can be measured as follows:

$$r(\mathbf{S}) = \max\left(1 - \frac{distance(r.m, r.n)}{r.l}, 0\right), \tag{1}$$

where $\mathbf{S}$ is a set of services that the user is currently utilizing. Accordingly, the spatio-cohesiveness of a user u and a set of services $\mathbf{S}$ can be calculated as follows:

$$cohesiveness(u, \mathbf{S}) = \sum_{s \in \mathbf{S}} \min_{r=(s, s_k, l)} \frac{r(\mathbf{S})}{|\mathbf{S} \cup \{u\}|} \tag{2}$$

This is the average of the minimum achievement of the requirement for each of the cooperating services.

To choose CPS services by considering whether the service effects can be consumed successfully by a user, we use the spatio-cohesiveness metric during the service selection process [3]. The spatio-cohesive service selection is performed continuously as the user moves in different spaces and/or as the availability of the services changes during runtime. In addition, a physical device for a service must be switched to an alternative device if its service effects cannot be cohesively delivered to the user. We call the process of switching a physical device to an alternative one for providing service effects in a continuous manner as *service handover* [3].

We developed a spatio-cohesive service selection algorithm by using reinforcement learning. The algorithm selects a set of services dynamically while simultaneously maximizing the spatio-cohesiveness and minimizing the number of service handovers [3]. We designed a reinforcement learning agent for dynamic service selection [3] and trained the agent by using the actor-critic algorithm [6].

3.3   Finding Cognitive Bugs in CPS Applications

In CPS environments, considering the manner in which the functionalities and effects produced by a CPS application affect user accomplishment of tasks is important. In particular, we can deepen the concept of user performance by studying cognitive resource utilization during Human Computer Interaction (HCI) tasks required by CPS applications.

We have developed an approach for analyzing the combination and/or sequence of application features that can optimize the use of cognitive resources of users. In particular, this method can find cognitive bugs that may cause cognitive interference and overload. For this type of testing, applying standard software testing techniques is not possible. Instead, models must be developed that emulate in the early stages of the software process the use of the applications. The use of cognitive resources must be assessed, and defining guidelines for a safe application design must be produced.

4   Preliminary Results

4.1   Testing Environment Prioritization

To evaluate the proposed environment-aware testing techniques, we conducted an experiment with a real-world application called "JQuery," which is a widely used JavaScript library. It can be installed on CPS devices that support JavaScript engines. We collected the build history of JQuery from JQuery's TestSwarm[1]. Forty-five builds that included the dates of the build history (ranging from 2017/12/13 to 2018/09/07) were contained in the build history data. For each build history, regression tests were performed under 16 test environments on average. Each test environment consisted of a web browser and an OS (both based on name and version). Forty-two builds included at least one failed test environment and at least one passed test environment, which means that at least one environment-specific failure in a build was possible. We used these 42 builds in the experiment.

---

[1] http://swarm.jquery.org/.

We measured the cost effectiveness of each test-environment prioritization technique by using $APFD_C$, which is a widely used measure in test-case prioritization studies [4]. We regarded a test environment as a test case when a test-environment prioritization technique was evaluated. The $APFD_C$ equation is as follows:

$$APFD_C = \frac{\sum_{i=1}^{m}(f_i \times (\sum_{j=C_i}^{n} t_j - \frac{1}{2}t_{C_i}))}{\sum_{i=1}^{n} t_i \times \sum_{i=1}^{m} f_i} \tag{3}$$

where n is the number of test environments, m is the number of failed test environments in a build, f_i is the severity of a failed test environment, t_i is the runtime in performing a test for a test environment, and C_i is the position at which failure i is detected in several test environments. $APFD_C$ values range from 0 to 100, where a higher $APFD_C$ means improved cost effectiveness. We assigned the same value (e.g., one) to the severity because we did not have information about the severity.

Figure 3 shows a result of the experiment. The X axis refers to the codes of the techniques, which are described in Table 1. The Y axis refers to $APFD_C$. Our techniques outperformed the baseline techniques (i.e., no ordering and random ordering). The $APFD_C$ of our test-environment techniques ranged from 85.05% to 91.70%, whereas $APFD_C$ of the baseline techniques ranged from 47.18% to 49.76%. Compared to no ordering and random ordering, improvement rates ranged from 37.87% to 44.52% and from 35.29% to 41.94%, respectively.

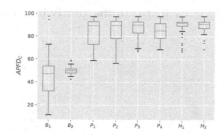

Fig. 3. Cost-effectiveness of the environment-aware testing techniques

4.2 Spatio-Cohesive Service Selection

To evaluate our spatio-cohesive service selection algorithm, we conducted experiments with simulated CPS environments. For each simulation, we instantiated a 100 m × 100 m area of the CPS environment and deployed 1000 CPS devices randomly. Each device had a capability of providing one of five possible services that the user required. We restricted the observation range of users to 10 m for a more practical simulation so that a user could observe CPS devices at a distance closer than 10 m. A user and the devices in an environment were mobile, each speed and direction were randomly assigned, and the maximum speed was restricted.

The maximum speed was set to $4\,\text{m/s}$, which was similar to that of slow vehicles in an urban space. Average spatio-cohesiveness over the simulation was calculated by identifying the spatio-cohesiveness for each selection step while penalizing for the number of handovers that occurred.

Our spatio-cohesive service selection algorithm was implemented by using Tensorflow[2], which is the most popular machine-learning framework. We compared our algorithm against three baseline algorithms: random, greedy-nearest, and greedy-handover, where the random baseline selects randomly, the greedy-nearest selects the nearest candidates, and the greedy-handover selects previously selected services until the services become unavailable.

Figure 4 shows a comparison of the average spatio-cohesiveness achieved by selection algorithms over 1000 simulations. For better visualization, we located circle markers for our algorithm, triangle markers for the greedy-handover, and rectangle markers for the greedy-nearest after every 150 simulations. The baseline for random selections showed poor performance as a result of the high penalty from numerous handovers. The baseline for greedy selections also suffered from the handover penalty caused by high dynamicity of the CPS environment. In the early phase of training, our algorithm showed a similar performance to the baseline algorithms in terms of average spatio-cohesiveness. However, our algorithm learned from experience and improved the selection policy iteratively. Specifically, it exceeded the performance of the baselines at approximately the 200th simulation and showed better performance in the late phase of training. Our algorithm achieved approximately two-to threefold the average spatio-cohesiveness compared to the greedy baselines.

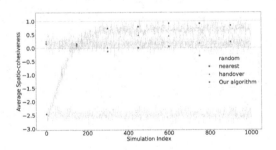

Fig. 4. Comparing spatio-cohesiveness of selection algorithms

4.3   Mental Workload Assessment

In human-centric CPS applications, accomplishing tasks is highly dependent on user performance. In our previous research [9], we addressed one of the main causes of low user performance, namely, multitasking. From cognitive psychology, we know that during multitasking, a user's cognitive resources (core assets used

---

[2] https://tensorflow.org/.

by cognition to perceive, think, remember, make decisions, and respond to the environment) are intensive, and this causes these resources to interfere with one another. Several studies have shown that weak cognitive interference can degrade user performance by 30%, and strong interference can stop an ongoing task. To avoid this type of inconvenience, in [9] we proposed a model to assess and classify mental workload, which is the explicit mental effort required to employ cognitive resources.

First, we developed an experimental design in which users performed six HCI tasks on a smartphone using Gmail and Tripadvisor applications. Users were simultaneously required to interact with their environments by performing physical activities such as walking and talking. This experimental design was based on the multiple resources model (MRM) of C. Wickens [12], which establishes the mechanisms of cognition for employing cognitive resources in different scenarios, such as during multitasking. Using an MRM model enables us to determine theoretically the number and intensity of cognitive interference and thus to establish different levels of mental demand. To collect data, we employed physiological sensors, surveys, and a video recorded by each user. In addition to data collection, we simulated the mental workload required by each task using the cognitive framework ACT-R [2]. We validated that the data simulated by ACT-R could be correlated with the real data collected by the sensors. This represented a major result because it showed that we were able to test CPS applications features in the early stages of the developmental process when no prototype of the system existed.

Second, we utilized the data from physiological sensors and ACT-R to create a machine learning model (support vector machine) to classify levels of mental workload. We placed special emphasis on the feature selection process, when we developed an algorithm that used both the aforementioned sources of data to improve the selection of features (CFS-SVM). The purpose of this algorithm was to increase the chances of selecting features from signal values that approximated simulation values.

With this model, we were able to classify two levels of mental workload with a 93.1% of accuracy on average for all tasks tested. We compared this result with a standard classification model that simply uses recursive feature elimination (RFE-SVM) to select features. Figure 5 shows the results of both models according five different tasks.

5 Related Work

Regression testing techniques for services have been previously studied [10,13]. Some studies have proposed regression test selection and test-case prioritization techniques for unit services, and other studies have considered test-case prioritization for a combination of multiple services (e.g., business processes). Our work focuses on testing services or a composite of services under various test environments, and we use test-environment prioritization techniques instead of test-case prioritization techniques to identify environment-specific faults as early as possible.

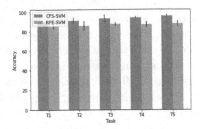

Fig. 5. Comparing models for different tasks

Most existing studies on dynamic service selection consider only traditional Quality of Service (QoS) attributes defined for web services such as availability, latency, and cost [11]. A dynamic service selection problem is commonly formulated as an optimization problem that makes selection decisions dynamically during runtime from among functionally equivalent services. When service selection algorithms from existing studies are applied for the purpose of selecting IoT services, the main limitation is that QoS metrics used in such studies cannot evaluate the physical characteristics of IoT services. Our study can address these limitations by using spatio-cohesiveness to locate IoT devices that are near the user to provide IoT services to that user.

6   Conclusion

A CPS application helps a user to accomplish a task in a successful manner by providing a set of necessary functionalities and/or by producing physical effects that are required to assist the user in his or her activities. In this study, we developed a software testing framework that ensures the reliability and safety of CPS applications that coordinate the various cyber-physical elements interacting in the users' environments and activities.

Our contributions can be summarized as follows. First, this is the first study that proposes a service-oriented CPS application framework by which CPS resources in different layers of the 5C architecture can be integrated while overcoming heterogeneity problems. Second, to improve the efficiency of testing CPS applications, we applied a regression testing technique that prioritizes various combinations of CPS environments. Third, we investigated a means of evaluating and selecting CPS services based on the effectiveness of delivering service effects to users through physical spaces. Finally, we developed an approach for analyzing different types and amount of cognitive resources that are required by a CPS application and human activities, and proposed a method of identifying cognitive bugs that may cause cognitive interference and overload.

We are currently developing a service-oriented CPS application framework that employs microservice technologies and a set of tools that can be used for DevOps activities. Our environment-aware software testing technique will be extended to practical CPS application domains and then further evaluated.

In addition, the models and algorithms for human-centric CPS testing will be enhanced by identifying and incorporating diverse situations and service effects that are directly and closely related to CPS applications.

References

1. Cyber-Physical Systems. https://www.nsf.gov/pubs/2008/nsf08611/nsf08611. htm. Accessed 25 Jan 2019
2. Anderson, J.R., Matessa, M., Lebiere, C.: ACT-R: a theory of higher level cognition and its relation to visual attention. Hum.-Comput. Interact. **12**(4), 439–462 (1997)
3. Baek, K.D., Ko, I.-Y.: Spatio-cohesive service selection using machine learning in dynamic IoT environments. In: Mikkonen, T., Klamma, R., Hernández, J. (eds.) ICWE 2018. LNCS, vol. 10845, pp. 366–374. Springer, Cham (2018). https://doi. org/10.1007/978-3-319-91662-0_30
4. Elbaum, S., Malishevsky, A., Rothermel, G.: Incorporating varying test costs and fault severities into test case prioritization. In: Proceedings of the 23rd International Conference on Software Engineering, pp. 329–338. IEEE Computer Society (2001)
5. Ko, I.Y., Ko, H.G., Molina, A.J., Kwon, J.H.: SoIoT: toward a user-centric IoT-based service framework. ACM Trans. Internet Technol. (TOIT) **16**(2), 8 (2016)
6. Konda, V.R., Tsitsiklis, J.N.: Actor-critic algorithms. In: Advances in Neural Information Processing Systems, pp. 1008–1014 (2000)
7. Kwon, J.H., Ko, I.Y., Rothermel, G.: Prioritizing browser environments for web application test execution. In: 2018 IEEE/ACM 40th International Conference on Software Engineering (ICSE), pp. 468–479. IEEE (2018)
8. Lee, J., Bagheri, B., Kao, H.A.: A cyber-physical systems architecture for industry 4.0-based manufacturing systems. Manuf. Lett. **3**, 18–23 (2015)
9. Lira, H., Ko, I.Y., Jimenez-Molina, A.: Mental workload assessment in smartphone multitasking users: a feature selection approach using physiological and simulated data. In: 2018 IEEE/WIC/ACM International Conference on Web Intelligence (WI), pp. 639–642. IEEE (2018)
10. Mei, L., Zhang, Z., Chan, W., Tse, T.: Test case prioritization for regression testing of service-oriented business applications. In: Proceedings of the 18th International Conference on World Wide Web, pp. 901–910. ACM (2009)
11. Moghaddam, M., Davis, J.G.: Service selection in web service composition: a comparative review of existing approaches. In: Bouguettaya, A., Sheng, Q., Daniel, F. (eds.) Web Services Foundations, pp. 321–346. Springer, New York (2014). https:// doi.org/10.1007/978-1-4614-7518-7_13
12. Wickens, C.D.: Multiple resources and mental workload. Hum. Factors **50**(3), 449–455 (2008)
13. Zhai, K., Jiang, B., Chan, W.: Prioritizing test cases for regression testing of location-based services: metrics, techniques, and case study. IEEE Trans. Serv. Comput. **7**(1), 54–67 (2014)

Author Index

Printed in the United States
By Bookmasters